Body Safety for Young Children

Empowering Caring Adults

by Kimberly King, MS Ed

Gryphon House
www.gryphonhouse.com

Copyright

Bulk Purchase

Gryphon House books are available for special premiums and sales promotions as well as for fund-raising use. Special editions or book excerpts also can be created to specifications. For details, call 800.638.0928.

Disclaimer

Gryphon House, Inc., cannot be held responsible for damage, mishap, or injury incurred during the use of or because of activities in this book. Appropriate and reasonable caution and adult supervision of children involved in activities and corresponding to the age and capability of each child involved are recommended at all times. Do not leave children unattended at any time. Observe safety and caution at all times.

This book is not intended to give legal, medical, or financial advice. All opinions contained herein are from the personal research and experience of the author and are intended as educational material. Seek the advice of a qualified professional before making legal, medical, or financial decisions.

Table of Contents

Dedication

This book is dedicated to my mom, Maryhelen Burk. An incredible mother, nurse, teacher, and passionate volunteer, you were a guiding light to us all. May you rest in heavenly peace and see all of your children and grandchildren continue your tradition of helping and serving others to make this world a better place.

Preface

I am delighted to introduce *Body Safety for Young Children: Empowering Caring Adults*, a vital guidebook for all those who care for children. As the founder of the Alexandra Gucci Children's Foundation, I believe that every child deserves to grow up feeling safe and secure, and this book provides a roadmap for how we can make that a reality.

As parents, caregivers, educators, and community members, we all have a responsibility to protect our children from harm and dangerous situations. Unfortunately, the world can be a dangerous place, and it's often difficult to know how to keep our little ones safe without instilling fear or anxiety in them. That's where this book comes in.

Body Safety for Young Children is a comprehensive guide to preventing abuse and empowering children to speak up if they ever feel uncomfortable or threatened. It features practical tips and exercises that adults can use to help teach these important lessons. It's an essential resource, not only for parents and guardians, but also for teachers, coaches, health-care professionals, and anyone else who works with children.

By taking an active role in promoting body safety, we can create a safer world for our children and ensure that they grow up healthy, happy, and free from harm. I am proud to support this important work and encourage everyone who cares about children's well-being to read this book and put its teachings into practice. Together, we can make a difference and create a world where all children can be safe and protected.

Warmly,

Alexandra Gucci Zarini
Alexandra Gucci Children's Foundation
https://www.alexandragucci.org/

Body Safety for Young Children: Empowering Caring Adults

Introduction

My Mess Is My Message

Truth: I'm an introvert who dislikes talking about herself. I'd rather listen to you talk about your battles with your toddler or commiserate with you about how the children in your classroom lose everything. I love to dig into significant issues and provide support. And only recently have I been comfortable enough to share my story more substantially.

When I talk with an adult about sexual-abuse prevention, fear often brushes across their face, and they want to exit stage right, find the door, or run. Sometimes, I forget that talking about protecting children from sexual predators is easy for me because I have been doing this work for eighteen years. But it is not easy for many parents, guardians, and teachers. They need a slow approach to the conversation on body safety. They need to dip their toe into the ocean. Many cannot just dive in; the waves are too big, and the water is murky.

Often, people fear diving into this topic because they are scared of what they might uncover. I want you to know that I was scared too! But, together, we will move past fear and empower our home and school families with support, knowledge, skills, and strategies that help prevent abuse.

Listen: At the end of the day, we are all doing our best. We also must learn as much as possible about sexual-abuse prevention to protect our children from harm. *Body Safety for Young Children* is a resource for caring adults who want to work together to protect children at a calm—not scary—pace. I will have to push out of my comfort zone to get this message to you in an authentic way. So, here we go. Deep breath.

My name is Kimberly King, and I am a survivor of sexual assault, a mom of three amazing kids, a sexual-abuse prevention advocate and certified Darkness to Light facilitator, a body-safety educator, and a kindergarten teacher. I'm also a certified K–6 teacher and have taught in schools worldwide, from Mississippi to Sicily. Talk about culture shock! *Mamma mia!*

I firmly believe the saying "Make your mess your message!" inspirational words from newscaster Robin Roberts's mother when Robin was trying to navigate her breast cancer diagnosis. Robin Roberts found motivation and clarity in her mother's words and decided to share her story with the intention to help others. With a great deal of guidance and support from my mindset coach, Jen Gottlieb, I have come to a place of certainty and understanding that *not* sharing my story with the world to help others would be a disservice. I had to get in that mindset to write this book. Thank you, Robin and Jen.

For you to understand my story, where I'm coming from, and how I can help you learn how to prevent sexual abuse and protect children, I need to share some personal things. We are going to have to get vulnerable here. I will not sugarcoat this issue because I know that will not serve you. This conversation requires us both to be authentic and vulnerable with the information. But before I start talking too much, I want to make sure you know what I am not: I am neither a doctor nor a therapist.

We all have to put down our fear and uncomfortable feelings on this subject. Understand that *not* talking about body safety and sexual-abuse prevention is what abusers want. They want us to be quiet. They want us to be uninformed and ignorant. They want us to keep secrets. We have to talk so that my mess doesn't become yours too. I believe that talking about sexual abuse is the key to preventing it. I have received thousands of emails and messages from families who have read my book and taken my online body-safety classes. I know this information saves lives.

The research is disturbing. Child sexual abuse is likely the most prevalent health problem children face with the most serious array of consequences (Townsend, 2013).

As parents and educators, we are in a unique and empowering position to prevent child sexual abuse and raise a generation of children free from childhood trauma and the physical and mental challenges that are consequences of abuse. The statistics and sheer magnitude of this problem are why I do what I do. I started off on this mission to prevent child sexual abuse with a goal of helping at least one child. I thought that my story was worth sharing if it could help one person. Let me tell you a few of the details so you can understand my motivation and why the work we will do in this space is so critical to child safety.

Some pages in this book may bring up memories or create distress. I encourage you to put the book down at any time. If you are triggered in any way, please know that you can step away, breathe, move, or phone a friend or therapist. Come back to this book tomorrow, next week, or when you are ready.

I hope you will engage with this book, with your thoughts and emotions, and with your family. So let's get to it!

My Back Story

I am the oldest of five children and grew up in a well-to-do family. We lived in a "good neighborhood," and the topic of sex and sexual-abuse prevention never came up. I had two loving and responsible parents. But back in the '70s, nobody even thought to talk about prevention. It wasn't on the radar. My parents thought we were safe and they did the best they could with what they knew at the time. They may have believed in a few common myths such as "That type of thing doesn't happen in this neighborhood or with our family."

Sexual-abuse prevention might have been a handy conversation to have had in more detail—especially after our babysitter tried to play show-and-tell with her bra and show my sister and me her boobies! We told our mom, and she made immediate adjustments to keep us safe.

I stumbled through high school having learned zero about sexual development and sex education, making many mistakes along the way. I left for college completely uneducated and unaware of how my body worked or about all things related to sex education.

If you are one of those people who didn't know the anatomically correct terms for your body or how everything functions until you were well into adulthood, I am your people. Didn't know what a clitoris was until you were twenty? I see you! I was utterly ill-equipped for the options and possibilities that would present themselves during my young adulthood.

My lack of knowledge left me extremely vulnerable. I would argue that sending your children to college or to live on their own without extensive sexual education and knowledge about sexual-abuse prevention is dangerous. For example, I had no idea someone might slip drugs into beer to knock a person out and have sex with them. Of course, that's not what this action is called. It's called rape. It took a long time for me to change that wording. Words matter and help you own your story. I hold that language now and acknowledge that it is part of my story.

When I called my mother to tell her that I had been a victim of sexual assault during my first week at the University of Maine, she told me I shouldn't tell anyone. She told me that no one would believe me. She told me that it would "ruin my reputation." I believed her! And she told me that I should just come home from school and try again next year. The feedback and opinions from my parents were upsetting. I carried that shame and guilt for thirty years. They didn't know any better.

But I didn't want to quit school. So, what does any intelligent girl who wants to get away from boys but also wants to stay at school in a circle of safety do? I joined a sorority. If you're unfamiliar with the process of "rushing" a sorority, it's a tradition in which women who are interested in sorority life attend social gatherings and events that allow prospective and current sorority members to get to know each other. The invitation that was slipped under my door that October was my golden ticket to safety! I left my dorm and moved into a sorority house called Pi Beta Phi. Suddenly, surrounded by a group of amazing women, I felt safe.

The icing on the cake was meeting our housemother—the person who manages the daily responsibilities of caring for a house and thirty young women and makes sure everyone is doing well. It took a lot to run a sorority house, and Sandy supervised it all. We all had jobs, and most of them were not glamorous. We cleaned our own bathrooms, washed the pots and pans, and raked leaves. Not only was Dr. Sandra Caron a wonderful housemother, she is one of the country's most distinguished professors of human development.

To this day, Dr. Caron is a role model, advocate, writer, educator, change-maker, mentor, and authority on all things sex education and sex development. I learned about human

Author (l) and Dr. Sandra Caron (r)

sexuality in her class. And, in a perfect full-circle moment, I have the honor of speaking at the University of Maine with her students every year to talk about body safety and empowering adults.

I'll never forget the first day of class! Dr. Caron walked in and said hello. Then, she began: "Let's talk about some slang words we use for our genitals. Boy parts first."

Two hundred college students stared at her or studied their shoes. Not. A. Sound.

She persisted: "Come on! I know we have at least a few to laugh at." Then, the slang words started flowing: *Johnson*, *Willy*, *Big Jim*, *noodle*, *weiner*—you get the gist! We continued with the terms for girl parts: *woo*, *cookie*, *China*, *'gina*, *honey pie*. The entire class was cracking up as she wrote about fifty terms on the chalkboard.

The point of the lesson was that we all needed to learn the correct terms because they are parts of the body. Dr. Caron explained that using slang or the wrong words can confuse other people. In the case of reporting a sexual assault, a person—especially a child—may report abuse to an adult, but that adult might not know their word for the body part that hurts or was touched or shown.

She assigned a term paper on the topic "What I Know about Sex and How I Learned It." I served as her teaching assistant that semester, and I learned a lot about sex by reading those term papers! Some stories were hysterically funny. Most of the students did not learn about sex from their parents. Many said they learned things from friends, older siblings or relatives, and magazines. (This was before the internet.)

The fun, learning, and curiosity I found as a teaching assistant pushed my trauma aside. But, that trauma crept up in waves. I had to do a deep dive to hide my mess. I did not want to think about what had happened that first week of school. I couldn't function with those thoughts. I blamed myself for drinking. I blamed myself for what happened. (Sound familiar?) I pushed all that trauma into a box, put it on a shelf, and tried to forget. About a quarter of the papers mentioned sexual abuse. Even though I learned through these college papers that I was not alone in my thoughts and feelings, it didn't help. I immersed myself in research, education, and volunteer work, and I started to heal by helping others. We each process trauma differently.

Take a minute to think about your history here. If these few paragraphs brought up any memories or triggers, write them down.

Gradually, the memories faded, and my engagement in helping women became my focus. For many years, I didn't even think about my assault until I had children. Specifically, my third child's birth was highly traumatic.

At the time, I was a Navy wife, and my husband was deployed. Soon after the birth, I needed to return to the hospital because my baby suffered complications from jaundice. I had to leave my two older children, ages six and four, with a neighbor friend and their family. At the hospital, I kept having a feeling that something was wrong. Have you ever experienced that knowing feeling? Do you just know in your gut, your heart, or wherever you feel anxious that something is wrong in your universe? Did you talk yourself out of it? Yes, I did that too! I was exhausted. I was running on fumes. I was happy to sleep in a recliner and have nurses bring me saltines and ginger ale. I talked myself right out of a whole bunch of feelings and decided that I was being paranoid. I convinced myself that my other two kids were okay and that I needed to sleep.

But it wasn't easy to sleep in the NICU (neonatal intensive care unit). My brand-new baby was sleeping soundly under a blue bilirubin light—the type used to treat newborn jaundice—but the hospital was too noisy for mom sleep. I got a cup of coffee and headed home to pick up my older kids. Exhausted, I drove to my friend's house, parked the car, and got out. As I started walking up the driveway, my son flew out of the front door like a rocket and ran toward me. He was upset. He jumped up into my arms, and I dropped my coffee. He hugged me and said, "Mom! I had a red flag."

My heart sank. Before the sleepover, I had taught my kids essential sexual-abuse prevention basics. I had told them that if anybody tried to look at, touch, tickle, or play with their private parts that it was a "red flag." (A red flag is a visual representation of the child's feelings of discomfort or fear. We talk more about this in chapter 2.) A red flag meant that this was an unsafe touch, and they should tell me immediately so that I could help them and keep them safe. We had talked about body parts, we had talked about body rules, and we had talked about telling.

As a young mom, I had no idea that an older child could do this to a younger child. I had pushed memories of our childhood babysitter and my distant thirteen-year-old cousin down deep. They had both been children abusing younger children. Instead, I had focused all my prevention strategies with my children on the strangers and the creepy guy in the white van. But this event shifted my thinking. My son's event caused this mom to go on a mission to prevent sexual abuse for all children. I started researching and looking for answers to help my child cope with the unsafe body boundary touch he had experienced during his sleepover.

I took my son to the doctor. He was no help.

I took my son to a therapist. He was no help. (My son's worries must have been boring because this guy fell asleep during our session. We slipped out the door and never went back.)

There were no books at the time that helped children and parents learn where the real risks were. I started to dig into the research and learned the facts and the resources. As it turns out, the chances that a stranger in a white van will sexually abuse a child are extremely low. I learned that most children are abused by people they already know, including friends and relatives. My son and I started journal writing and talking about body safety and sexual-abuse prevention. Our thoughts and conversations in our journal entries became the basis of the book *I Said NO! A Kid-to-Kid Guide to Keeping Private Parts Private*. I became a Darkness to Light facilitator and prevention specialist.

That's the pretty, prepackaged, press-release story I told the world.

But the truth is that I was still scared to talk about it. My son's experience triggered an emotional avalanche for me. It triggered memories from my childhood, of the sexual assault in college, and of how my issues at school were handled. I spent a lot of time crying in the shower (which is an excellent place for a kid-free mini breakdown).

I was a mess. A big, giant, hot dumpster fire of a mess.

> "A powerful way to shift the shame from the past is to speak your truth in the present."
>
> — *Gabrielle Bernstein,*
> **Happy Days**

I had to seek therapy at this point because I couldn't handle it any longer by myself. I was alone, a military wife with three kids (one of whom was a new baby), a deployed husband, and a family eight hours away. My trauma could not stay up on that shelf a moment longer. So I sought care and help from my doctor and a therapist. I joined a support group. I started going to hot yoga. I told my sisters my story. And I started talking about my mess, which has now become my message.

My intention for sharing all of this information in this book is to try to prevent you from having your own mess. If you already have your own mess and there is some sexual abuse in your past, I hope this book will inspire and assist you in helping your children learn how to avoid situations and seek help when needed.

What This Book Is

This book is a primer or guide to help adults empower and protect the children they love and care for. The intention here is to bring awareness, research, statistics, and authentic communication around the topic of body safety and prevention, with a collaborative twist. I want this book to make the topic of body safety as easy to talk about as discussing bike helmets or buckling up.

This book can help adults learn how to identify a "red flag" in a risky situation or a behavior. The material is organized in a logical way that helps present the information in a commonsense flow. We start by reviewing some basic statistics and facts. Then, we move into identifying grooming behaviors and developing body-safety strategies and skills that minimize the risks and empower families. This book helps adults drop the fear over this tough topic and protect children. Every child deserves a safe, healthy childhood free from trauma.

This book is not:

- full of fluff or fake in any way.

- for survivors who are looking to heal from past trauma.

- intended to give any medical, therapeutic, or legal advice.

I am an expert of my own story. I am a survivor. And I am sharing my knowledge and experience.

I know that parents, guardians, and teachers are essential partners in this prevention mission. I want caring adults to be on the same page so they can be effective and can reinforce skills and strategies together. Children spend 90 percent of their time with their moms, dads, other adult family members, and teachers. We are the most important people in children's lives. We have to learn how to protect children. This book is an easy-to-use reference and guide for both home and school.

We all have something in common and something to share. I have been where you are in some way.

I'm the oldest of my siblings.

I'm a parent.

I'm a teacher.

I'm a daughter.

I love my three children with all of my heart.

I'm divorced.

I'm a fierce advocate for all children, especially those who have passed through my kindergarten classroom doors.

I'm a survivor!

Many of my friends are survivors!

I've been a champion for children all around the world.

I'm an introvert, a mama bear, and a fan of coffee and wine.

I'm a giver and a helper.

I want you to learn how to effectively protect children from sexual abuse for a lifetime. I am writing this book for you. This book is the most important one I can write and you can read to further this goal. I am honored to serve you as a parent coach, a mom friend, a body-safety expert, a teacher, a facilitator, or whatever you want to call me. I look forward to sharing lessons learned and personal stories, and I encourage you to share yours with others. Because when we talk about sexual abuse, we help to prevent it. Parents, guardians, and teachers are our children's best advocates. So, let's move forward and work to prevent sexual abuse.

Chapter 1

It's Not the "Man in the White Van"

I was so paranoid as a new mom, which was probably residual trauma from my childhood showing up as hypervigilance. (Thank you, Gabby B.) I was worried about everything. I had seen one too many *CSI* episodes, and I was sure that my daughter would be kidnapped out of her bedroom window by a man in a white van. You know, that middle-aged creepy white guy with the puppy and candy. I had the whole house safety proofed before my daughter was born.

We bring our memories and trauma surrounding the topic of safety with us as women, as young parents or guardians, and as teachers. Because of my history, I became extra safety cautious. I became known as a "safety freak" by my husband and eventually by my children. I took this as a term of endearment, but it was actually a way for some to poke fun at me through the years.

One of the biggest misconceptions many adults have, myself included, is the idea of the man in the van. We fear strangers and tend to teach children not to talk to them. But the man in the white van, the stranger, is not typically the person who poses the most significant risk to a child. There are exceptions, of course, such as the case of Elizabeth Smart. Elizabeth actually was kidnapped by a "man with a van," who climbed up a ladder, opened her window, forced her out, kidnapped her, and sexually abused her for months. But the family did know of him. He was not a total stranger. He had done work on the house weeks before.

Most child sexual abuse comes from the people we know and trust (Finkelhor and Shattuck, 2012). These are the people in our circles: close family, more distant relatives, babysitters, coaches, teachers, and religious leaders. Wherever there are children, abusers go. Abusers are also online, and the COVID-19 pandemic created a situation where predators are very aware of where our children are—and how much information they share. We'll talk about grooming more in chapter 2.

To be super clear, let's add an excellent definition of child sexual abuse. Clarity prevents confusion. As I mentioned in the introduction, I am a Darkness to Light–certified Stewards of Children facilitator (https://www.d2l.org). We use the following definition to explain child sexual abuse in our workshops and trainings:

> Child sexual abuse includes any sexual act between an adult and a minor, or between two minors, when one exerts power over the other, such as forcing, coercing, or persuading a child to engage in any type of sexual act including non-contact acts such as exhibitionism, exposure to pornography, voyeurism, and communicating in a sexual manner by phone or internet (Townsend, 2013).

The Rape, Abuse, and Incest National Network (RAINN, 2023) gets a little more specific by including more examples of behaviors:

- Exposing oneself to a child

- Masturbation in the presence of a minor

- Forcing the minor to masturbate

- Obscene conversations, phone calls, text messages, or digital interaction

- Producing, owning, or sharing pornographic images or movies of children

- Sex of any kind with a minor, including vaginal, oral, or anal

- Sex trafficking

- Any other contact of a sexual nature that involves a minor

Before we continue, I want to dispel common myths so we can all be on the same page.

Fourteen Fabulously `False` Misconceptions about Child Sexual Abuse

1. **It's the man in the white van.** Ninety percent of child sexual abuse happens within the inner circle of trust, including family members and the people we already know (Finkelhor and Shattuck, 2012). While it is essential to teach children that the safest practice is to only talk to strangers when they are with a trusted adult, stranger danger is often overemphasized.

2. **Only girls are at risk for sexual abuse.** One in four girls and one in six boys will be sexually abused before age eighteen (Townsend, Rheingold, and Haviland, 2016).

3. **Children will tell when they are abused.** Only 26 percent of survivors of child sexual abuse disclose their abuse to adults, and 12 percent disclose to the authorities (Bottoms, Rudnick, and Epstein, 2007; Lahtinen et al., 2018). A shocking fact is that the majority of children never tell anybody. There is overwhelming evidence that most child victims delay disclosing or never disclose sexual abuse to friends, family, or the authorities (Bottoms, Rudnick, and Epstein, 2007).

4. **All teachers are safe adults.** In the past, I have taught my students and families that teachers are safe adults. But that is only true in some cases. Predators are attracted to teaching because it is a position, time, and opportunity with children.

5. **Children can't sexually abuse other children.** That's a super-false myth. Sadly, 40 percent of sexual abuse comes from child-to-child abuse. Older, more powerful children can prey on younger or smaller children (Finkelhor and Shattuck, 2012). This type of abuse goes under the radar all the time. A more recent study puts the percentages much higher at about 70 percent (Gewirtz-Meydan and Finkelhor, 2020).

6. **Siblings don't abuse each other sexually.** That is a myth. Child-to-child sexual abuse in the family between siblings is a taboo topic that nobody talks about, and it is thought to be the most common form of intrafamily abuse, perhaps up to three times as common as sexual abuse of a child by a parent (Krienert and Walsh,

2011). According to Jane Epstein, a survivor of sibling sexual abuse, activist, and cofounder of 5 Waves (https://www.5waves.org), "Sibling sexual abuse is still the most taboo topic to talk about and is rarely reported."

7. **It's too late to teach sexual-abuse prevention.** It is never too late to teach children about body safety. You can start when they're two, or you can start when they're seventeen. Ideally, it is better to start early, but what is important is that you start.

8. **Teaching children about body safety with books is all I need to do.** I'm going to read a few books to them, and I'm done. They'll be able to fight off a predator and take care of themselves. That is entirely false. A small part of sexual-abuse prevention is reading books. But, that is not enough. A comprehensive strategy and family safety plan, which we will discuss later in the book, involves learning the facts and statistics and implementing body-safe choices. Teaching about body safety should happen calmly, constantly, and continuously because the content changes as children grow. There is no way a child will be able to ward off a skilled predator just by reading a couple of books on body safety. As parents, guardians, and teachers, we must make safe choices regarding what our children do and whom they spend time with, both online and off.

9. **The internet is safe for children as long as they are supervised.** Absolutely false. The internet is not safe for children, even if you're supervising. Children can bump into an incredible amount of inappropriate content that can damage and traumatize them. Also, children can repeat what they see innocently. This applies to all things children can access online, including video games and cartoons. Provocative and inappropriate videos can give children ideas that they don't understand. Young children may reenact these activities or actions with other children in person at school, on playdates, or at sleepovers.

10. **Having a cellphone makes my child safer.** Drop the mic, drop the phone! That smartphone puts your child in front of every online predator. If you can do one thing today, don't let your child have one. (We'll look at alternatives in chapter 7.)

11. **Posting pictures of my child or my students online and elsewhere is okay and safe.** Posting a child's face, your pictures, your location, your school, or identifying language, whether online, on a child's T-shirt, or on a school bumper sticker, is entirely unsafe. Predators are looking for children and for their location. Even

if a school has a policy and permission slips to allow teachers or administrators to share marketing and social posts online, I would opt out of participating in that activity. That one picture of a bunch of cute preschoolers with their school logo and tagged location gives a predator an exact location of a perfect possible target. Photos can become usable and shareable. A picture can be screenshot, manipulated, and used for personal gratification and extortion.

12. **Playdates are safe.** Playdates are not safe just because you know the family. You never know the level of observation and supervision a friend will provide for your child. There is no way of knowing how advanced or completely ill-equipped your friend, their children, and anybody else in their house is regarding body safety. Are there older children in the home? Are the doors to the bedrooms closed? Are the children always observable? If something goes wrong, will your friend call you? Do your friends and everybody in that household know about body safety, and do they enforce body-safety rules for a safe playdate?

13. **Sexual abuse doesn't happen in our neighborhood.** Sexual abusers do not discriminate. It can and does happen daily in any neighborhood, house, culture, religion, and socioeconomic status. It happened in my neighborhood, it happened to me, and it can happen in your neighborhood. That might be hard to hear, but it is true.

14. **Sex education is body safety.** Not exactly. Sex education is not body safety, but body safety is a tiny part of the beginnings of sexual education. Body safety involves simple strategies for children, parents, guardians, teachers, and all who care for children. It starts by using the correct body terms and teaching body autonomy. In body-safety education, we learn that private parts have unique rules, and we encourage communication with our safe adults and families. We focus on feelings, communication, and consent. Nowhere in body-safety education do we talk about actual sex, reproduction, sexual relationships, or sexuality. However, there is nothing wrong with talking about sex with your own children at whatever age you are comfortable with. You know your child best! I wish my mother had at least told me something about sex before I was sixteen. Sex-education curriculum starts for children around third or fourth grade in most schools. Some parents talk about sex and sex education with their children at home to a certain extent, but there are gaps in the education on this topic. This is why talking about body safety early and often during childhood is critical.

These are myths that apply to children in the early childhood setting. But they change as children grow and move toward discussions on sexual education. As young people grow up, conversations change from body safety, body autonomy, body boundaries, rules, and safe adults to conversations about consent, body-part function, sex, and sexuality.

Parents or guardians must be their child's first source of communication on all things related to body safety. You don't want your child googling sex! You don't want your child learning about things from their friends or on YouTube. Getting comfortable from the start on body safety will make the more uncomfortable topics easier to talk about by the time your child is seven. You don't want your child accidentally falling into a conversation with a predator on social media platforms.

You *do* want your child to be confident to talk with you about this topic. Let's change these misconceptions and work together to educate children.

Take a minute to write down some common myths that might have taken up space in your head.

The Other 10 Percent: Strangers

Now that you know that children who are sexually abused are—by an overwhelming margin—abused by somebody they already know or trust, what about the other 10 percent? There are still dangerous strangers and people who snatch and grab both children and adults. There are folks who may have slipped through the system and still pose a serious threat to our safety.

In a 2022 Las Vegas carjacking, a heroic nine-year-old girl saved her baby brother and escaped a kidnapping by using her words, manners, and negotiation skills. She managed to convince the carjacker to let her go. She grabbed her baby brother and ran barefoot back to find her mom and get help. Imagine how terrified this little girl and family must have been.

✗ ✗ ✗

In certain situations, even when we do everything right, we may still find ourselves in danger.

Many of us have taken self-defense courses because of this, and we use our cellphones to help track our movements. Often women go out in groups, avoid walking alone in parking lots, and are aware of our surroundings. I carry pepper spray in my purse. How about you? In chapter 11, we will explore how to prepare children—without scaring them—to make an emergency exit.

In the next chapters, we will dig in and dig deep. We will unpack the essential sexual-abuse prevention strategies and skills that you need to protect the children you love. So, get ready, take a deep breath, and get comfortable with being a little bit uncomfortable. How do predators gain access to children? What tricks do they use? Let's rip the bandage off and learn how to spot the red flags of grooming behavior.

Chapter 2

Spotting Red-Flag Grooming Behaviors

Now that you know that most child sexual abuse comes from the people we know and trust (Finkelhor and Shattuck, 2012), let's consider the tactics that predators often use to groom children. What is *grooming*? Well, it is not making sure your child is clean and practices proper hygiene. In this case we are talking about sexual grooming of a child by an abuser. Child grooming is a deliberate, planned, manipulative set of behaviors abusers use to gain access to a family and child for the purpose of developing a secret, sexually abusive relationship with the target child.

According to Darkness to Light (2023), grooming "allows offenders to slowly overcome natural boundaries long before sexual abuse occurs. On the surface, grooming a child can look like a close relationship between the offending adult, the targeted child, and (potentially) the child's caregivers. The grooming process is often misleading because the offender may be well-known or highly regarded in the community. As a result, it's easy to trust them." Often, sexual predators groom an entire family and gain trust and access before they even lay a hand on the child. If you know what to look out for, you may have a chance to identify a risky person before anything traumatic happens.

As parents and educators, we want to keep children safe from harm. We teach them to wash their hands, cover their mouths when they cough, buckle their seat belts, and always wear helmets when riding a bike. Sexual-abuse prevention is a bit more complicated than that, but it doesn't have to be scary or difficult. The good news is that parents, guardians, educators, and children can be empowered by investing a minimal amount of time in education about sexual-abuse prevention. Learning about prevention can help adults protect children immediately.

Red-Flag Tactics of Abusers

Sexual predators come in all shapes and sizes. They can be men or women. Statistically speaking, 90 percent of child sexual abuse is committed by men and those known to the child (Finkelhor, 1994; Finkelhor and Shattuck, 2012). Most schools, camps, and other youth organizations are full of wonderful, dedicated adults who care about children. But, because these are places where children spend a great deal of time, the settings can attract predators. I recommend every school and organization that cares for children create and enforce a sexual-abuse prevention policy.

What Are the Red Flags?

So, what are the questions we need to ask schools and organizations that care for children?

- Does the organization have a sexual-abuse prevention mission statement?

- Are the teachers and staff required to know the policy and procedures for preventing sexual abuse?

- Does the school have required training for all staff?

- What is the screening process for teachers and staff?

- What is the screening process for school volunteers?

- Does the school practice the rule of two (always having two adults present with children)? A child should never be alone with one adult.

In addition, as a parent, caregiver, or professional, ask the following:

- Is there a school employee who does parents favors frequently? For instance, does the person volunteer to watch children after school as extra child care?

- Is there a school employee who is overly friendly with a child and refers to the child as their favorite student or special friend?

- Is there a school employee who invites a child to their home after school?

- Is there anybody at school who hugs and touches children without asking for consent?

- Is there anybody at school who asks a child to keep secrets?

- Is there anybody who makes a child feel uncomfortable?

- Is there anybody at school who gives you a funny feeling or a bad vibe?

- Is there an adult who sends home special gifts just for a particular child?

- Is there an adult who is trying really hard to get close to the adults in a family?

- Is there an easy way for a child to report all forms of abuse?

Abusers have methods to choose and manipulate victims through various techniques and tricks. They try to gain the child's and family's trust first and eventually will move toward grooming. Our job as proactive parents, guardians, or teachers is to learn the facts about sexual abuse, minimize the risk, and teach children about safety. One thing all abusers must have is access to children. The following are some red-flag phrases and tactics abusers may use.

"CAN YOU KEEP A SECRET?"

Tactic: Secrecy

Sexual abuse thrives under layers of secrets. If a child hears this question from an adult, it is a *huge* red flag. A skilled abuser may ask a child to keep an innocent secret, such as "Let's keep this treat our little secret. Don't tell your mom we got ice cream before dinner." The initial secrets are small and benign, seemingly harmless. A teacher, coach, or any respected authority figure who asks a child to keep a secret would be a cause for concern.

When the predator is confident the child has kept benign secrets, they will move on to acts of sexual abuse, demanding secrecy about that behavior. At that point, the child may feel so guilty and ashamed that they feel they cannot tell.

What you can do: Implement a no-secrets rule. Tell young children they must never keep secrets from their parents or guardians. Some children may accept this as a rule; others may be curious and ask why. A simple answer is that secrets can be dangerous for children, and caregivers always want to know the truth so they can always help children. Or, explain that, while most adults are good, there are tricky adults with bad intentions who try to trick or hurt children.

Children can get confused about the difference between secrets and surprises. A few years ago, my illustrator and I created this short, animated video to help children understand. The video explains the difference between secrets and surprises and describes how the adults who want to keep children safe would never ask them to keep a secret. You can watch the video here: https://bit.ly/3Kupnri

"YOU'RE MY SPECIAL FRIEND."

Tactic: Friendship

Abusers try to build relationships with children by promoting common interests. They also try to establish trust with children by making them feel special or unique. An abuser will try to gain the affection of their intended victim by sharing these interests and things they have in common. If a teacher, coach, or any adult caregiver tries to become a child's friend, this is cause for alarm.

What you can do: Remember that children need age-appropriate friends, and adults need adult friends. Communicate and connect with children about boundaries and rules.

Related: "The 3 Big Red Flags of Sexual Abuse" (King, 2016)
https://www.defendyoungminds.com/post/3-big-red-flags-sexual-abuse

"LET'S SPEND SOME QUALITY ALONE TIME TOGETHER."

Tactic: Isolation

A big red flag! Adults have adult friends, not "special" child friends. Any activity requiring an adult to be alone with a child is unsafe, especially overnight. Abusers try to normalize certain behaviors and lower inhibitions. A situation in which a child must change clothing or do a sleepover, such as a hiking trip or a church retreat, is inherently risky. If a teacher or coach is offering to give a child rides home or provide child care in isolation, this is a red flag.

What you can do: Don't let children spend time with adult "friends," not even your own adult friends. Implement the rule of three: there should always be at least three people present—one adult and two or more children or two adults and one child.

"DOES SOMEBODY NEED A HUG?"

Tactic: Affection

Pats on the back, a hug to say goodbye—these may be completely acceptable actions in many circumstances. Because of this, many predators seek careers with easy access to children. Affectionate gestures and touch may seem benign, but these behaviors can be a way for an abuser to normalize touch before moving to a sexual touch. Teachers must be careful here. I know some teachers who take the topic of touch so seriously they refuse to have any touch, which I think is sad. Sometimes a young child wants to hold their teacher's hand or give her a morning hug. It is essential to remember that we never want to assume that a child wants a hug or a pat on the back. Be sure to ask for consent before giving the child that hug. This is an excellent way to model consent and help your students develop body autonomy.

Tip: Be aware of a child's reactions to other adults and comfort levels regarding physical affection. Does the child avoid certain people?

What you can do: Teach children to tell a parent, guardian, or other safe adult if they ever feel uncomfortable about any physical contact. Ask if anybody makes them feel uncomfortable with affection. Learn about consent, and teach body autonomy to children from an early age.

"I CAN BABYSIT FOR YOU."

Tactic: Free Services and Gifts

Predators also may present as a person who is showing up for a parent or guardian and child by offering free services. For example, "I know you can't afford guitar lessons right now, so I will do it for free." Granted, some free classes and services are offered out of the kindness of perfectly good people. But, most adults in business do not offer to do things for free. If the free service or lesson includes isolating a child, be careful. Private guitar lessons, tutoring, babysitting—any activity in which a person tries to have one-on-one time with a child is a red flag. Some children who play video games receive free gifts from strangers online. This is also something all parents need to discuss with their children. Gift giving from a person for no apparent reason without parental permission is a big red flag.

What you can do: Ask to sit in on guitar lessons or go with your child to tutoring. Sit outside an open door, and listen and observe. Talk with your child about gift giving and receiving; talk about when it is appropriate to accept gifts and from whom. Gift giving as a form of grooming can happen over a period of years, before any touch or uncomfortable feelings happen.

One survivor shared, "My grandfather gave me extra everything! He always bought me little presents and took me to do special things. He started having me sleep over a lot because my parents were in the middle of separating. By the time I was seven, my grandfather was my favorite person in the world. He saved me from the turmoil on my house. By the time I was eight, the touching started and it quickly turned to sexual abuse. I realize now that my grandfather groomed me for years and that he also made me feel that I caused him to act this way. He blamed me for the abuse. He said I was his favorite and that I accepted all his gifts and generosity, therefore it was my fault."

"YOU'RE THE BEST ONE ON THE TEAM."

Tactic: Ego Boosting

Predators enjoy building up a child and a targeted family with ego-boosting compliments. This can happen in a subtle fashion in public, private, and online to adults and children. Children as young as four have access to iPads, and some children play video games online as well. Online grooming happens in these spaces.

What you can do: Be extra careful with your children and the access you provide to online games. Limit their use of tablets and cellphones. Build your child's self-esteem from within the family. Daily, communicate about feelings and activities that help your child feel valued and appreciated. Even something as small as, "Honey, I love this piece of artwork you did at preschool! Tell me about how you made this. You worked so hard on this! I am so proud of you and your creativity. Let's hang this up right away." You can't do enough building of self-esteem and positive self-image work. Building emotionally secure kids who love and respect themselves is the goal. Helping children know their self-worth protects them.

Praise, praise, praise your children as often as possible—not just on how cute they are but on how kind, loving, thoughtful, helpful, and important they are. You want your children to confide in you when they have wonderful days and share in the joy of their childhood. You also want them to trust you enough to tell you their troubles. Look out for the ego stroker, and pay attention when you notice one.

"WANT TO HEAR A DIRTY JOKE?"

Tactic: Humor

An abuser can lure a child closer by using jokes and games. These may start with G-rated jokes, but those soon lead to "dirty" jokes, showing children online pornography, or introducing sexual games. Part of the grooming process is trying to normalize sexual language and activity. Normalizing sexual activity can happen in person and online. A predator may send explicit materials through social media apps and video games. They may ask for or demand inappropriate photos from a child. Children can easily feel trapped and scared in this predicament. What is alarming is how it starts with a liked post or a hello and seems harmless. These master manipulators can easily trick both children and adults.

What you can do: If a child is old enough to have internet access, parents and guardians should monitor emails, texts, video games, and social network messages. Talk about online safety and show a child how a person might try to trick children. For example, explain that a tricky person can set up a mock profile on a social media app and pretend to be another child. It is easy for anybody to set up a profile with a fake age and photo and to use a filter that changes their appearance. Explain to children how adults also can have fake profiles on video games and pose as children. The most important thing to stress for young children is that they should never be online alone or without a safe adult supervising. Learning how to operate safety online starts with constant supervision and communication. Parents and guardians, consider installing apps such as Bark to help protect and monitor your child. (Note: We take a closer look at apps in chapter 7.)

Teachers, it's great to be light and fun with students when the time is right. But, keep jokes and communication appropriate. If students bring their phones to class and share locations and identifying information, such as school, grade, after-school activities, teams, and so on, they put everyone at risk. As a teacher, I recommend requiring your students to turn off their phones and place them in a basket on your desk or in a pocket on a cellphone check-in chart. Make sure to remind your students that you are an advocate for their learning, health, and safety. Make it easy for them to share with you any online problems or safety problems by keeping a conference mailbox on your desk. This is a simple mailbox where students can slip you a note if they need help with a safety problem and need to speak with you privately.

Communication is vital here. Let children know that if they make any mistake they should tell you, and you will support and help in a judgment-free zone.

"YOUR PARENTS DON'T UNDERSTAND YOU. I KNOW HOW YOU FEEL."

Tactic: Empathy

Sometimes, children feel isolated or alone, especially during family duress. Separations, divorce, or other changes in family structure or location can make children more vulnerable. A simple, "I know how you feel. My parents fought a lot too!" can be all is needed for a young person to connect with and confide in a predator. Family structure, such as a non-nuclear family structure, or problems within the family are reported to be risk factors for child sexual abuse (Assink et al., 2019). The risk increases when children live with stepparents or a single parent. Children who live with a single parent who has a live-in partner are at the highest risk: they are twenty times more likely to be victims of child sexual abuse than children living with both biological parents (Sedlak et al., 2010). Abusers target single moms for this reason. Children living without either parent (foster children) are ten times more likely to be sexually abused than children who live with both biological parents (Sedlak et al., 2010).

What you can do: I believe that the biggest risk reducer of all is empowering caring adults to prevent child sexual abuse. Regardless of your family structure, if your family does go through a stressful period, pay attention. A great family counselor can help get ahead of some of these issues. Be extremely careful of introducing new people to the children. Do not invite new partners or friends to have unsupervised access to your children. Don't let new partners or friends sleep over when the children are home. Make sure you have discussed body safety with your children and have a list of safe adults.

"YOUR PARENTS WILL NEVER FORGIVE YOU IF THEY FIND OUT WHAT WE DID. YOU DIDN'T SAY NO!"

Tactic: Shame

A child is not able to give consent in a sexual relationship. And the blame-and-shame control game is hard to handle. A predator will use a child's confusion and fear as they attempt to maintain control over the victim by saying statements such as, "You wanted this. You liked it too. It was your idea!" or "If you tell, your parents will be so ashamed of you!" or "If you tell your mom, you will ruin our whole family and I will go to jail." This tactic is common in a child-on-child abuse situation as well.

Cathy Studer (2019), award-winning author and sexual-abuse prevention advocate, shares, "My perpetrator was my stepfather, and the abuse lasted for six years, from age six to age twelve. I didn't tell anyone, as my shame was too great. My stepfather told me the abuse was because I was bad and this was my punishment. I came close a few times to talking to my mom. Yet, I didn't because I was afraid of how she would respond. My stepfather told me that my mom wanted him to punish me in this way when she was at work at night. . . . In most cases, it is so incredibly hard for children to share what is happening because the shame is so great. The longer the abuse happens, the more the shame builds. Many perpetrators also threaten that if a child tells, there will be a breakup in the family unit, putting the burden of sharing and that fear on the child."

What you can do: Children need to know that no matter how long any inappropriate contact or abuse has gone on, it is **never** their fault. They need to know that their safe adult, parent, or guardian will always help, protect, and love them. Review with children that it is always okay to tell and that you will always believe them.

"LET'S PLAY THE POCKET GAME."

Tactic: Normalizing/Desensitizing

An abuser will desensitize a child to touching and discussion of sexual topics. For example, an abuser might start to touch the child in ways that appear harmless, such as hugging, tickling, and close dancing, and will later escalate to increasingly more sexual contact. Predators will use games that include hiding objects or money in underpants, massages, and asking to shower at the same time. Abusers may also show the victim pornography or take children to sexually explicit shows or movies. They may encourage sexual topics with them in a fun setting to introduce the idea of sexual contact.

What you can do: Review body-safety rules and body boundaries. Encourage children to tell their parents, guardians, or another trusted adult if anything like this ever happens. Remind them you are a safe adult and will help them. All children must know that sexual abuse is never a child's fault. Remind your children and students that we never play games with private parts because it breaks our body-safety rules. Cathy Studer (2019) shares, "I can honestly say that if someone would have taught me, first and foremost, that I had body boundaries and the ability to say no to uncomfortable touch, that would have made a big difference in me opening up about the abuse sooner."

"IT'S NORMAL! EVERYONE WATCHES NAKED VIDEOS WITH THEIR FRIENDS.

Tactic: Inclusion

Abusers like to make their behavior seem normal to avoid concern. Phrases such as "Everyone does it," or "It's what most kids do" are red flags.

What can you do: Be alert for signs that a child has a relationship with an adult that includes secrecy, controlling behavior, being overly touchy, giving money or gifts, and sneaking around.

Have constant and ongoing communications about body safety and consent at every age. Talk to children about healthy, appropriate relationships with peers.

"I'M SORRY YOUR DAD LEFT. I AM HERE FOR YOU AND YOUR MOM."

Tactic: Void Filling

Single moms (and sometimes dads), watch out for this one! I am in no way blaming you for getting divorced. Heck, I have been divorced twice and had to be careful with my choices too. I made plenty of really bad decisions. There are wonderful men and women out there who are good people and are not child molesters. However, predators use the super-subtle and extremely risky tactic of void filling. If you are aware of this tactic, you will notice it and avoid it immediately.

Researchers Elliott, Browne, and Kilcoyne (1995) say that perpetrators report that they look for passive, quiet, troubled, lonely children from single-parent or broken homes. Predators often target single parents for a variety of reasons. Many newly divorced people are processing a life change. Some are sad, depressed, and lonely, while others may be living their best life, going out with friends, making risky decisions, and hiring a lot of babysitters. Both types of behavior are attractive to sexual predators, who may use grooming strategies on the parent to gain trust. For example, a predator might offer free child care or rides for children to sports practice or dance class or might encourage the parent to go out with her friends or go to yoga or therapy while they watch the children. An abuser might even offer take the children for a weekend so the parent can go on a getaway with her girlfriends. Abusers need time and access. While a predator is grooming the family, they gain access by being needed and filling a void.

What can you do: Refrain from dating for at least a year if you can. It takes a lot of emotional processing and recovery to heal from the trauma of a divorce. Children need time to accept, understand, grieve, process, and adjust to a completely new family structure and routine. This time can be difficult for families. If you can wait, focus on yourself, your mental health and wellness, and the children. You need to be strong, confident, and levelheaded before you start investing your time and emotions into a new relationship. And, your children need to have the time to process the difficult emotions around a divorce. Building the family, focusing on togetherness, and developing new family traditions that encourage self-esteem will protect your entire family in the long run and will make your family a less attractive target. Spend time doing family activities that encourage love, acceptance, and compassion, which will help protect your children for years to come.

When you do decide to date, look for information on about your dates online, check their social media accounts, and consider getting a background check. Court records are public, so you can request a name-based record check from your local clerk of court. There is a fee for this service, and you would have to do this for each county where you believe the person has lived. You can also check your state's sex offender registry online. Unfortunately, most sexual predators are never caught, so background checks and offender registries will only show the small percentage of people who have been caught and charged.

Ask to meet former romantic partners. Meet the person's family and friends. Ask for and check the date's references. You can never be too safe here. Feel free to be "that mom" or "that partner." Keep your dates out of your home. Do not let them sleep over; sleep at the other person's house or leave the children with their other parent. Don't accept any free services from a new adult friend such as babysitting or rides to sports practice or music lessons. Don't accept favors or extra presents for your children. Don't let your children spend any alone time with a new adult until you have built a lasting, trusting relationship.

✗ ✗ ✗

I know this sounds a little over the top, but part of my work in preventing child sexual abuse involves working primarily with single moms. (And I am still a single mom.) They call me for individual counseling on prevention strategies. I also run a group for moms who have been grooming victims and have experienced having a new partner sexually abuse their children. This is a serious risk and can be prevented through education and implementing safe strategies and choices. If you are going to be a "safety freak," this is an excellent place to focus. You can make all the difference.

Parents and guardians have the immense responsibility of protecting their families from sexual abuse. The best way to add a layer of protection is to educate yourself and your children about sexual abuse. Sexual abuse can be prevented when caring adults learn the facts and minimize the risks for the family.

Chapter 3

Safe Adults and Safety Circles

A circle of safety is a way to surround yourself and your children with safe adults. In the book my son and I wrote, *I Said NO!* (2020), I define safe adults as aunts, uncles, grandparents, firefighters, police officers, teachers, emergency medical technicians, and 911 operators. But this definition is flawed because we know that 90 percent of child sexual abuse happens with people in our trusted circle, such as relatives, friends, older children, and pillars of the community.

So, how do we redefine *safe adults*? I am in the middle of publishing a new edition of *I Said NO!* with Brandylane Publishers. In it, I change some of the language I use to be clearer and more accurate.

Aunts can be safe. But, not all aunts are safe.

Uncles can be safe. But, not all uncles are safe.

Grandparents can be safe. But, not all grandparents are safe.

Firefighters can be safe. But, not all firefighters are safe.

Police officers can be safe. But, not all police officers are safe.

Teachers can be safe. But, not all teachers are safe.

You get my drift? My new definition of a safe adult is about the adult's behavior. A safe adult behaves in specific ways. For example, a safe adult would never:

- ask a child to keep any secrets from a parent or guardian.

- ask a child to lie.

- ask a child to break a body-safety rule.

- ask a child to do anything that made the child upset or uncomfortable.

- bribe, trick, or blackmail a child into doing anything.

- threaten a child in any way.

- use mean, aggressive, or sexual language.

- ask a child for inappropriate pictures.

- claim to be a child's "special friend."

- buy a child things that their parents or guardians don't know about.

- try to spend extra alone time with a child.

Adults who do these types of things are unsafe!

Build Your Family Safety Circle

How do you figure out who the safe adults are in your circle? When your child is young and unable to express whom they feel safe with, you will have to use your best judgment based on the facts, risks, and your gut instincts. As your child grows, who do you trust to pick up the phone when the child calls for help? Who would pick up your child if they were in danger? Who would be available to talk with your child if the child has a problem?

Who are the people in your life whom you know will protect your child and want to learn about body safety? Grandma was my safe adult. But, in your safety circle, Grandma might not know the signs and symptoms of child sexual abuse or even know how to handle a disclosure of sexual abuse from a child. So, anybody you ask to be in your safety circle will need a little training and must be willing to communicate with you and your child. A member of your safety circle needs to be invited in and made aware of the responsibility involved. Ideally, many conversations on the topic of prevention will happen within your family and safety circle as your child grows.

Parents can start talking about body safety and their prevention efforts with teachers, child-care providers, babysitters, family, doctors, and everyone who interacts with their children. Letting everyone you know that you are well-versed in sexual-abuse prevention will help protect your children. Including others in your efforts will create a ripple effect, thus protecting more children.

As children become more aware of their emotions and are able to communicate, you can start having safety chats. Try to assess whom your children feel the most comfortable and happy with. Ask them questions about their teachers, grandparents, aunts, teachers, babysitters, and so on. These would be the people your little one would feel safe with if they had to get picked up because of a stomach bug or potty accident at school.

A simple and easy way for parents to introduce the topic of safety to family, friends, teachers, and care providers is to send a letter explaining what you teach your children about body safety and red flags. Another strategy is to donate a body-safety library to your school, your child's classroom, and your public library. Or, volunteer to come to class and read the a few child-friendly body safety books to the students. Consider asking the school parent organization to bring in a body-safety speaker to empower the adults and protect the children from child sexual abuse.

People who are in our safety circle can also be called "green-flag people." I use the red and green flag system in my book *I Said NO!* For young children, this can work well because they are learning colors and may associate the color red with stop signs, warning signs, or red lights. They may associate green with *go*. If *safe adult* and *unsafe adult* are terms that seem too abstract for your little one, try incorporating the color red for unsafe adult and green for safe adult. Take a minute to ask your child if they know any unsafe adults. Write down the details.

What Teachers Can Do

At the beginning of every school year, I start an individual file for each child with vital information including their full name, birthday, parents, custody schedules, cell numbers, emails, and an emergency contact list. I encourage parents and guardians to talk with their children about this list. Ask them who should be on it and why. And ask them who should *not* be on the list and why. These questions can be very revealing and sometimes funny. For example, my brother was not allowed to be on our safe-adult list because Uncle Shenton was a "bad driver who got parking tickets." (Something my children must have overheard me say. Oops.)

One great way to encourage communication between the educators and parents or guardians is to use journals. A simple notebook can go with each child back and forth from school to home. Every year, each child in my kindergarten class gets an old-fashioned journal with their name on it. Every day they are at school they come in and do a journal entry. The entry may be a picture or a few beginning words. I usually share writing prompts for my students to assess their mood. At the bottom of each page I add a check in:

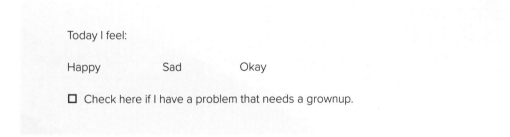

Today I feel:

Happy   Sad   Okay

☐ Check here if I have a problem that needs a grownup.

Every night at home, they use this same journal to write about what happened after school. They can take a photo, draw a picture, or write a few words or a sentence. At the bottom of the home page are notes from parents or guardians. There, a child's adults can let me know if there were any issues such as problems with sleep, being upset from the previous day, problems with friends, and so on. A communication journal encourages reading, writing, learning, communication, identifying feelings, and talking about problem with adults on a daily basis. It's an old-fashioned win-win! And if children consider it "homework," they will do it!

I recommend to families that they try their own communication journal at home. This can be a fun way to get the entire family involved in talking about feelings and sharing. Simply buy a notebook and on each page write a question. Each family member can answer the question of the day in the journal, and the family can talk about it or read about it after dinner.

Most of my kindergarten students make safety-circle lists as part of our general safety discussions at the beginning of school. A typical list will include Mom, Grandma, Dad, a best friend, a pet, and me! It's important to explain to children that safe adults have to be older than eighteen and human. (Adult humans have a much better chance of reacting responsibly and getting a child to safety. Although my therapy dog, Alfie, is trained to alert for medical crises and does other tasks such as barking at the mailman, he just doesn't make the list.) I explain to all of my students that I am a safe adult at school. So, if they have a problem, feel uncomfortable, or feel unsafe, they can talk to me or tell me anything. But, I can't really pick them up from soccer practice if they twist an ankle.

WHAT TO DO IF A CHILD DISCLOSES A PROBLEM

- Thank the child for telling you.

- Listen.

- Tell the child you are proud of them for telling, and remind them it is not their fault.

- Keep your cool.

- Provide support, and don't ask too many questions.

- Once you have gathered enough information, make the appropriate phone calls to ensure the child's safety.

Above all, try not to freak out. Freaking out and getting upset in front a child may cause the child to recant or stop sharing. In front of the child, don't threaten to harm or hurt the abuser. Many children are abused by people they love, and this can cause feelings fear, shame, guilt. It may even stop a report in its tracks because some children want to protect the abuser from harm.

Babysitter Safety

Some babysitters are perfectly safe, but not all babysitters are safe adults. Babysitters can pose safety concerns for many parents and guardians. The stereotypical babysitter is a teenage girl who cares for neighborhood children to make a little extra money (not to be confused with a nanny, who is a professional caregiver). Both babysitters and nannies pose a risk because they have time alone with your children. We often think that only men perpetrate sexual abuse, but that is a myth; babysitting or nannying is where the female predator may show up. We tend to let our guard down with babysitters and even with some female teachers, because females are often judged as less of a threat than males. The thought of a woman abusing a child can seem hard to fathom, but the truth is that sexual abuse by females happens and is highly underreported and often perceived differently due to gender stereotypes, media, movies, songs, and concepts of masculinity. Female-perpetrated sexual abuse is often confused by young children with ordinary, day-to-day care.

According to a comprehensive study on female perpetrators of child sexual abuse, researchers Ashling Bourke and colleagues (2014) found that approximately 6 percent of all the victims of child sexual abuse in the sample were abused by a lone female. Analyses indicated that male- and female-perpetrated abuse differ. Female perpetrators are more likely to be younger than male perpetrators. Females are more likely to abuse male victims and older children and adolescents (age 9–17 years), compared with male perpetrators. In addition, female perpetrators are less likely to be a stranger to the victim and in a position of authority (Bourke et al., 2014).

The risk of sexual abuse by a female is not extremely high, but it is still a risk. As a culture, we tend to trust women and judge them as less sexual or aggressive. These gender-biased stereotypes can lead parents and guardians to quickly form trusting relationships with babysitters and other female caregivers.

Please remember that 40 percent of child sexual abuse is committed by older, more powerful children (Finkelhor and Shattuck, 2012). This can include your fourteen-year-old neighbor who babysits your children or your fifteen-year-old cousin who is visiting from out of town and volunteers to babysit.

> When I was six and my sister was four, we had a family friend babysit us so my parents could go out to dinner. "Angie" was fifteen and had

babysat us a few times. She let us stay up past our bedtime and let us eat ice cream before bed. She let us watch TV! And she asked us to keep all these secrets from our parents so that we could keep on having fun. I was six. I didn't know that all of these fun things could actually lead to anything bad.

After a few months of secret keeping, Angie went for the inappropriate sexual move during bath time. She showed us her bra. She tried to get my sister and me to touch her breasts. She tried to get us to play a touching game with her. We were instantly scared and worried. My sister and I made what we now refer to as an "exit strategy." We dried off and put our pajamas on. My sister Kathy pretended to feel sick and said she was going to throw up. Angie quickly moved away from us and went to watch TV.

I knew the name of the restaurant where my parents were. I found the take-out menu and dialed the number. I told the pizza man we had an emergency and gave him my parents' names. My mom and dad were home within twenty minutes, and our ordeal with Angie was over.

After this experience, we made a safety plan with our mom. We all agreed that our neighbor Mrs. Granata would be our safe adult and our safety spot. Usually, our grandma babysat us, or we slept at our grandparents' house when our parents went out. Unfortunately, however, Angie was not our last bad experience with a babysitter.

A couple of years later, our parents let a fourteen-year-old distant cousin babysit us. Almost from the moment they pulled out of the driveway, he started making inappropriate suggestions. "Do you guys want to play a game? All the teenagers play Seven Minutes of Heaven in the closet!" My sister and I knew that didn't sound good! "Do you want to play Married in your parents' bed? I always play Married when I go to friends' houses. It's a really fun game. We just take off our clothes and roll around in the bed like the grownups do. It's fun!"

He didn't know that we already knew about private parts and safety. We told him we had to pee, and we ran out the back door. Mrs. Granata called our parents. We were safe. The next day, he was forced to apologize to us and brought us a giant stuffed animal to show his regret. We refused the stuffed animal. We never saw him again. I often wonder what happened to him and if he went on the sexually abuse other children. As a sexual-abuse prevention educator, I imagine something must have happened to him when he was younger. And, I know from other sources that he had done this type of thing before.

The last babysitter I remember was a woman named Fannie. She was about sixty-five years old. There was no funny business with Fannie; she ran a tight ship. We followed all the rules and there were no secrets. I can still remember the last thing she said to me:

"Girls, your mama told me what happened with the other babysitters. Something like that happened to me too. And I want to tell you the rule I tell my kids and grandkids. Babysitters are only ever allowed to touch one part of your body: your feet."

We both exclaimed, "What? Your feet? Why? That's weird!"

Fannie walked over with a warm washcloth and asked, "Is it okay if I clean your feet?" We agreed. She told us that feet are always dirty after a long day of playing. She said we should wash our feet to keep our sheets clean and to make less work for our mom. She was right—our feet were filthy. She tucked us in and we had a safe, carefree night.

Establishing sexual-abuse prevention policies and family safety plans goes a long way here. (We'll look at creating a family safety plan in chapter 4.) An excellent solution to the babysitter "what-ifs" is to make a policy, discuss it with all of your babysitters, and post it on the refrigerator. Family safety rules for babysitters or care providers can change with the children's ages and needs. You can also have a family meeting before you leave your child in the care of a babysitter to review the rules.

HIRING A BABYSITTER

Don't just hire a babysitter off of Facebook or post an ad on social media or Craigslist. That is a giant red flag! Instead, before you hire a sitter, do the following:

- **Do an extensive background check.** Start by asking your prospective babysitter or nanny to submit to a background check. You will need permission and personal information such as full name, driver's license number, and addresses. Some babysitter sites such as Care.com require sitters and care providers to complete background checks before they can be connected with families. You can also check your babysitter's driving and arrest records through your state's public records website. Also check the registered sex offender website for your state.

- **Ask for and check personal references carefully.** Make sure the references are not family members or close friends. Ask some serious questions about the babysitter, such as:

  ▸ How did your children like this sitter?

  ▸ Did they have any complaints?

  ▸ Were there any problems?

  ▸ Did the sitter play with the children?

  ▸ Did the sitter follow your rules?

  ▸ Was the sitter late?

  ▸ Was the sitter flexible?

  ▸ Did you have any disagreements?

- **Review the sitter's online presence.** Look at their social media posts. Google the sitter's name.

- **Do a trial run.** Set up a mother's helper playdate or two so you can observe the babysitter with the children and watch for red flags. (A helper playdate means having the sitter watch your children for little while you are also at home doing other tasks.) After the trial run, talk to your children about the babysitter. Ask your children whether they liked the sitter. What fun things did the sitter do with them? If the sitter seems okay so far, have them keep your children for three hours during a day. Pop back in and out frequently, between errands, so the babysitter is not sure when you might be there.

- If you think the sitter might be suitable, share all of your sexual-abuse prevention books and rules with them and have the babysitter sign a family safety contract.

- If you can, install security cameras in your home.

- When you do have the babysitter watch your children, check in frequently.

Babysitter Body-Safety Contract

I, _____ , understand and agree to the following terms as part of the family safety plan for the protection of the children in my care.

1. I will always maintain appropriate physical boundaries with the children in my care. I will never engage in inappropriate or suggestive behavior, and I will not touch any child in an inappropriate or uncomfortable way.

2. I understand that it is my responsibility to prevent any type of abuse from happening to the children in my care. I will immediately report any suspected abuse or inappropriate behavior to the child's parents or legal guardians.

3. I will never take any photographs or videos of the children in my care that could be considered inappropriate or compromising. If the parents/legal guardians request photos or videos, I will take only appropriate and respectful photos or videos and share them in a manner that is safe and appropriate.

4. I will always listen to the children in my care and take their concerns seriously. If a child discloses any type of abuse or inappropriate behavior to me, I will believe them and report it immediately to the child's parents or legal guardians.

5. I understand that I am a mandatory reporter of suspected abuse or neglect of children. If I have any suspicions or concerns about the safety or well-being of a child in my care, I will report it immediately to the appropriate authorities.

I agree to abide by the terms of the body-safety contract as part of the family safety plan. I understand that this contract is for the protection of the children in my care, and I take it seriously.

Signed: _____

Date: _____

Family Safety Rules for Babysitters

Design your own Family Safety Rules based on the ages of your children. The following is an example of some language to include:

Our children are educated on sexual-abuse prevention.

Our children have body autonomy and are not forced to hug people.

Our children are not allowed to be alone in their rooms unsupervised.

Our children do not take baths or showers unless their parents [guardians] are home.

Our children do not need help going to the bathroom (depending on age and potty-training level of success).

If our children are uncomfortable or have a problem, you are responsible for calling us or contacting a person on our family safety plan if you cannot contact us.

Our phone number is _____. You can call us at any time! Our safe adults' phone numbers are _____ _____. If you cannot reach us, please call these numbers.

Do not take photos or video of our children at all.

Turn off your location on your cellphone while you babysit.

Limit cellphone use while you are watching our children.

Our children do not keep secrets.

Parent/guardian signature: _____

Babysitter signature: _____

✗ ✗ ✗

You are off to a great start here! We have already covered so many important topics. We have learned about the some of the myths and dug in to some of the facts that relate to reducing the risk for young children in general. All of which lead up to the how-tos of actually building a family safety plan. Now is a great time to move around, take a walk, and then do a little journal writing to jot down any thoughts you have swirling in your head. You may have many great ideas brewing on how to make your home or classroom a safer place. In the next chapter we will discuss the why, what, when, who, and how of developing a family safety plan. My goal is to empower you with many useful strategies and skills you can implement today.

Chapter 4

Family Safety Plans

While developing a family safety plan can seem like an overwhelming task, it can be broken down into small parts that start with a conversation about how to protect your children. As a certified Stewards of Children Facilitator with Darkness to Light, I know how important it is to reduce the risk of child sexual abuse and educate the adults.

Think about the circumstances and opportunities you have as a parent or guardian to create protective circumstances and make situations safer. You need to be thinking in a proactive way to get ahead of the problems that could happen. Think about all situations that could pose a risk, from babysitters to playdates to cousins to preschool. Find ways to minimize the risks to your children by implementing safety strategies. For instance, we already know that child-to-child abuse accounts for a great deal of child sexual abuse. So, before you agree to a playdate at your child's new bestie's house, take a few extra steps.

Get to know the parents or guardians, the family, and the child. Invite the new friend and parent or guardian over to your house or to a neutral site such as a playground first. Talk about what you have learned about body safety thus far. Share some books. Ask some questions. Once you have had time to host a few playdates and feel comfortable with the new friend, and once communication levels between you and the new friend's parent or guardian are solid, you can consider trying a playdate at the friend's house. Try going over for coffee with your child and stay at the playdate to chat with the parent or guardian.

Take a few minutes to be proactive. Think like a prevention specialist. Some questions to ask yourself as you are assessing the situation:

- Can I see the children from where I'm sitting/standing?

- Who else is in the home?

- Are there any siblings?

- Are the children playing in open spaces?

- Are there any household rules posted?

- Is there a general feeling of calm?

- How does the caregiver handle disagreements and problems?

- Do the children have access to the internet?

- Do the children have access to cellphones, tablets, and computers?

- What types of shows are the children watching?

- Are there planned activities?

- Is there a safe and observable place for the children to play outside?

Once you have made an internal assessment of the new friend, the family, and the environment, know that it is okay to ask questions. When it comes to discussing concerns about body safety, approach the conversation with sensitivity and empathy. You do not want to step on a perfectly lovely parent's or caregiver's toes and offend anybody. A few tips:

- **Use "I" statements:** When expressing your concerns, focus on how you feel and what you have observed. This will help you avoid making the parent or guardian feel defensive or attacked. For example, "I noticed that your son was uncomfortable when his older brother was wrestling with him, and I wanted to talk to you about your thoughts in that."

- **Focus on the children's well-being:** Emphasize that your concerns are rooted in a desire to protect the children's safety and well-being. Remind the parent or guardian that it is important to have open and honest conversations about body safety to help prevent abuse from happening.

- **Offer resources:** Provide the parent or guardian with resources, such as books, articles, or videos, that can help educate them on body safety and how to talk to their children about it. This can help them feel more empowered and informed and less lectured or judged.

- **Use a collaborative approach:** Instead of telling the parent or guardian what to do, work together to develop a plan for how to address any concerns or issues related to body safety. This can help the parent or guardian feel more involved and supported.

- **Be sensitive to cultural or personal beliefs:** Keep in mind that different families may have different beliefs or cultural norms around body safety. Be respectful of these differences and try to find ways to accommodate them while still prioritizing the children's safety.

- **Use compassion:** It is important to approach these conversations with compassion and understanding in a judgment-free zone.

Remember that your goal is to work together to create a safe and supportive environment for the children. You can ask the parent or guardian how they will observe the children. Will they play in the bedroom? outside? in the basement? And how will the parent or guardian handle problems? Will they check in on the children frequently? Will they call you if needed? These questions might seem alarming, but it's better to be a little "extra" as my kids call it. It's better to be "that mom" asking all of those questions upfront than it is to play catch-up after there is a playdate mishap, problem, or scary situation. (And remember to listen to those internal thoughts and feelings. If the situation doesn't feel right and you are feeling strange and uncomfortable, or if you see any red flags, it's okay to cancel or leave.)

After the playdate, check in with the parent or guardian. Asked how it went and if there were any problems. And, I always recommend asking your child how the playdate was.

You have to be a little creative here, because you might just get, "It was fine!" Try, for example:

- What was the most fun thing you did with your friend?

- Did you do anything that made you super happy?

- Did you make anything?

- Did you play any new games?

- Did you do anything silly that made you laugh a lot?

- Did you feel safe?

- Did anything happen that made anybody sad or mad?

- Did anybody get in trouble?

- What was the best part of the playdate?

- What was the worst part of the playdate?

Encouraging communication after all situations in which your children are not with you is important.

Talking about body safety plans with children, friends, teachers, and family members does not have to be scary. It can be one of the best gifts you give them—the ability to speak up and find their voice. Building your child's self-esteem and confidence are the steppingstones to nurturing strong and empowered children.

Amy Nguyen, Deputy Director of Research at Darkness to Light, shares that there are some protective factors to consider when developing safety plans. She agrees with Bethell et al. (2019) that "[p]rotective factors or positive childhood experiences can aid children in having healthy development and mitigate the effects of child sexual abuse and other adverse childhood experiences." Protective factors for children can include:

- Feeling comfortable to discuss emotions and feelings with family

- Having a supportive family through tough times

- Enjoyment in participating in community activities and traditions

- Feeling a sense of belonging at school

- Having a supportive group of friends

- Having a safe adult who has a genuine interest in them

- Feeling safe and protected by an adult in their home (Bethell et al., 2019)

All of these factors help children develop a sense of belonging and secure attachments. Children feel loved, supported, and confident when you are mindful as a parent, teacher, or caregiver who directly contributes to a child's emotional development in a positive and meaningful way. I hope you realize how critical your role is. Providing safe, loving, kind, confidence-building, and healthy learning and growing environments has a powerful ripple effect for their safety in the short and long term. Having a family that is well versed in body safety and sexual-abuse prevention strategies can protect them even further.

Code Words

As part of your family safety plan, you will need to decide on a code word that your children can use to immediately alert you that they are in danger or are uncomfortable. When you agree upon a code word, it means that your child will say or text the code word, and you will come immediately without asking any questions. You can ask questions later when you get your child to safety, but if your child calls you and says the code word—for example, the word *spaghetti*—you respond, "I will be right there." And you retrieve your child from wherever they are.

A code word is useful, for example, if your child is at a sleepover party. If your child calls you or texts you at two in the morning with the code word, your response is, "I'm on the way." Code words are essential because sometimes children are embarrassed to make a phone call in front of friends or other people to alert a parent or caregiver about a particularly uncomfortable or unsafe situation. They may be worried about what their peers are thinking. They might be concerned about being ridiculed. Or they might be worried about the problem getting worse.

Code words can be helpful for all sorts of situations, not just about body safety. For example, if your child is being bullied at a playdate and feels uncomfortable and wants to leave, they can use the code word for that situation. If something is going wrong with a babysitter, your child can text or call you with the code word, and you can come home. You can also share the code word with your safety circle of safe adults.

I teach the parents in my online training classes that code words are really useful when their child has a red-flag feeling. When a child feels unsafe, uncomfortable, or is having a body safety problem, they would raise a red flag to the situation in their head. For example, the child may think, "I don't like playing this game. I feel weird. It's a red flag." Then, the child would implement the code word soon after, calling or texting mom or dad and using the code word. Of course, the child can also simply say or text, "I had a red flag! Please come pick me up." We talk more about red-flag situations in chapter 2.

Once you have developed your family safety plan, post your family's body-safety rules on the fridge and in the bedrooms to help with prevention. If you have a babysitter or friends over, they will see that body safety is on your radar. Remember, an educated and empowered child is an unattractive target for an abuser.

The "No Secrets" Rule

Secrets are dangerous, no matter how you try to spin them! And they are hard for children to understand. When secrets are surprises, they are planned to make someone happy and bring joy.

An excellent example of this is a surprise birthday party. But secrets are just not that simple.

A skilled predator will use secrets to determine whether a potential victim might be manipulated.

A child can find themselves trapped in a sticky web of secrets in no time at all.

Secret keeping is an easily overlooked part of the grooming process. An abuser's technique can be pretty slick as they methodically groom a child over time. For example, the predator may first ask a child to keep a secret that seems innocent, saying things like, "Let's keep this treat our little secret." or "Don't tell your mom we got ice cream." These are testing secrets. A predator will test your child to see if they will keep a small secret. Teach your child that if they hear a phrase like "Don't tell your mom," or "Let's keep this our little secret," they should raise a red flag in their heads and tell you right away. We talk more about the importance of identifying feelings and communication in chapter 9).

Then, when the abuser is sure the child has kept that secret, he will move on to bigger secrets and slowly move toward acts of sexual abuse, demanding secrecy there as well. At this point, the child may feel so guilty, ashamed, and scared that they think they cannot tell. In my Body Boss Bootcamp, and in the *I Said NO!* book, I teach children that a red-flag secret is a secret about a private part. If somebody asks a child to keep a red-flag secret, they should tell a safe adult right away. When somebody says, "Don't tell your mom," I train children, "Tell your mom."

Take a peek at my video "Red Flag Secrets" on YouTube.com. (https://www.youtube.com/watch?v=r4BnCGAIj5E) It may help you explain this tricky topic to children.

Some important facts about disclosure worth noting are that one third of child sexual abuse incidents are identified, and even fewer are actually reported. Researchers estimate that 38 percent of child victims disclose the fact that they have been sexually abused (London et al., 2005; Ullman, 2007). Of these, 40 percent tell a close friend rather than a safe adult or authority figure (Broman-Fulks et al., 2007). When children report abuse to friends and not to safe adults, these reports can go nowhere. This means that the vast majority of child sexual abuse incidents are never reported to authorities, though research suggests that disclosure rates to authorities may be increasing (Finkelhor and Shattuck, 2012).

Sadly, according to many child protective service agencies, about half of the child sexual abuse incidents reported to them are investigated. The rest are "screened out" for lack of adequate information or for other reasons (Block and Williams, 2019). Sexual abuse thrives in isolation, lack of awareness, lack of education, silence, and secrets. A no-secrets policy coupled with an ongoing conversation about safety is critical. Open communication and education are essential in keeping children safe.

7 Simple Strategies That Can Help Protect Children from Grooming Techniques

1. **Review body boundaries and consent.** Begin by teaching anatomically correct body part terms, body boundaries, and consent. Teach children that only a few people (such as parents or guardians, caregivers, or doctors) under certain circumstances (such help with hygiene or supervised checkups) can see their private parts. Otherwise, nobody is allowed to see or touch their private parts. Nobody is allowed to ask them to see or touch other people's private parts.

   Abusers use touching games to test for reactions as part of the grooming process. Tickling is not a safe touch. Be on the lookout for any tricks such as tickling in private areas. Nobody is allowed to ask them to keep a secret about private parts! That's a red-flag secret.

2. **Teach children they must never keep red-flag secrets.** If an adult or friend violates their body boundaries, teach children that they must go to a safe adult immediately.

3. **Red-flag secrets are never a child's fault.** Let children know you will always believe them; it is not their fault. They will not be in trouble for telling you they had a red flag.

4. **Get help from your safety circle.** Children may be too scared or embarrassed to talk to you if they need to report sexual abuse or an inappropriate situation. Parents and guardians, teach your children about three additional adults they can contact in red-flag situations. Make sure you know and trust these adults to act responsibly.

5. **Children need to know that red-flag people lie!** Abusers use lies, bribes, and tricks to keep children quiet. Remind children that if a person asks them to keep a secret about their private parts and says, "You can't tell anyone," that is not true. They can and must tell a safe adult.

6. **Brainstorm with children lies a red-flag person might say that could trick them into keeping secrets.** For example:

    "You are special. Let's keep this our secret."

    "If you keep our secret, I will bring you a treat."

    "If you keep this secret, I will give you money."

    "If you tell, nobody will believe you."

    "If you tell, your parents will be mad at you."

    "If you tell, I will say it was your idea."

    To protect and prepare your kids, rehearse scenarios and responses to these events.

7. **It is never too late to tell.** Remind children that even if they have been keeping a red-flag secret for a long time, it is never, ever too late to tell. Make sure children know that a red flag is never their fault! They should feel comfortable telling you anything and trust that you will believe them, no matter what. Encourage open communication, trust, support, and a judgment-free zone.

    If a child does reveal an abusive incident, as upsetting as it may be, try to remain as calm and supportive as you can manage. That will encourage the child to speak freely and will avoid the possibility of compounding a child's fear or shame.

✗ ✗ ✗

Family safety planning is a critical part of an effective sexual-abuse prevention plan when paired with a protective philosophy that makes talking about body safety as normal as talking about buckling up in the car or putting babies in car seats. Safe adults who make it possible to tell, make it easy to tell, and ask questions create a safety net. Telling can happen and the statistics on prevention and reporting can change. Ideally, when children are brought up in an environment where body safety is the focus, prevention can happen, and reporting won't be needed.

But nothing is foolproof. There are circumstances beyond our control, and that is why knowing the signs and empowering our children with the tools to tell are key. One of the building blocks of body safety starts by learning what is "normal" in child development, sex, sexual development, and sexuality. Because, let's face it, children can do some pretty strange, silly, goofy, and confusing things. In the next chapter, we will talk about some of the common questions about curiosity and child development.

Chapter 5

Is This Normal? Common Questions about Child Behavior

"Curiosity is natural. When young children discover that they are different, curiosity and exploratory behavior are natural responses. By accepting children's natural curiosity about sexuality and gender differences as normal and healthy, parents build a basis for positive attitudes toward sexuality."

—Sandra Caron, **Professor of Family Relations and Human Sexuality, University of Maine**

Children need touch and affection to bond with their parents or caregivers and develop into healthy adults. They need warmth, encouragement, love, and kindness. Without touch and affection, children fail to thrive and their brain development is affected (Ardiel and Rankin, 2010). Attachment is one specific aspect of the relationship between a child and caregiver that is involved with making the child feel safe, secure, and protected (Bowlby, 1982; Mooney, 2010). The purpose of attachment is not to play with or entertain the child; this would be the role of the parent as a playmate. It is not simply feeding the child; this would be the role of the parent as a caregiver. Neither is it setting limits for the child; this would be the role of the parent as a disciplinarian. It is not teaching the child new skills; this would be the role of the parent as a teacher. Attachment is when the child uses the primary caregiver as a secure base from which to explore and, when necessary, as a haven of safety and a source of comfort (Waters and Cummings, 2000).

Teachers can play a critical role here as they spend precious time with children in these formative years. A child needs to attach to at least one parent or caregiver to form a healthy bond and develop in a secure and healthy way. When children do not get enough attention, affection, time, or love, or if they are neglected, abused, or in distress, they crave attention and sometimes seek it in the wrong places. Children under stress or dealing with depression and anxiety, family discord or broken homes, school isolation, or bullying can be starving for love and attention.

A negative self-image or lack of positive self-esteem can put a child at risk. Expert abusers can find these children and easily manipulate them, particularly when they have online access to them. These children are at high risk for online grooming. (More on that later.)

Healthy touch and secure attachment are essential in normal child development. Children need hugs, snuggles, and kisses from their important adults at bedtime. They also crave time, love, and care from their teachers. Sometimes, they need to hold your hand for that extra bit of support. They need you to put a bandage on that boo-boo if they fall off a bike. These behaviors are normal because they are motivated by love, care, health, and hygiene.

The other side of the healthy-touch coin is that we need to normalize consent and respect the body boundaries of children. Always ask for a hug. Have conversations about body boundaries and a child's body rights. These child-development goals and conversations help develop a sense of self and a positive self-esteem in children. They will feel supported, loved, and cared for, which are essential in helping children be healthy and well-adjusted.

So What Is "Normal" Behavior for Children Ages Three to Five?

Let's face it! Children do some weird things at home and school. As a mom of three very different children, I believe it is fair to say that there is a vast spectrum of "normal" behavior. This book focuses on behaviors that might be problematic for parents and caregivers and may indicate sexual abuse—although, sometimes not! And please remember: I am coming at this from the angle of mom of three, veteran kindergarten teacher, and sexual-abuse prevention educator, author, and advocate. I am not a doctor. So, if you see abnormal behavior that is out of the ordinary for your child, always follow your instincts, ask questions, and seek professional help from a pediatrician, therapist, or child-advocacy center. What is "normal" for your children might not have been "normal" for mine. When mixed with different personalities and parenting styles "normal" behavior is on a spectrum.

Take a minute to write down some of the weirdest things your children or the children you teach have said or done.

Curiosity is normal. Young children look at naked bodies and run around naked. They ask questions all day long. They can frequently have their hands in their pants. Exploration, masturbation, potty humor, playing doctor—all normal.

You are the expert on your own children and the best person to figure out when your child is acting abnormally. Teachers, you spend lots of time with children and have a unique perspective on each of them. Educators are trained to observe, notice, question, and engage. For example, a teacher might notice something with a child's behavior that is suddenly different. Having healthy communication between home and school can make it easier to identify and communicate about many problems quickly.

I have seen and heard some pretty wild and silly things in kindergarten, but I have witnessed some dangerous behavior as well. Regarding body safety and prevention, we must learn the signs of sexual abuse and assess children constantly. For this chapter, we are going to examine what may or may not be considered normal "sexual" activity. However, in my opinion, young children are not sexual—they are curious. They are exploring sensations and their bodies, which is typical of children this age.

By preschool, many children have a stable sense of gender identity. Typically, children of this age are not concerned with gender pronouns, sex, sexuality, or labels.

A wonderfully unique group of children passes through my classroom every year, and each year is different. Teaching is never dull! Each year, I get questions from parents, teachers, and children about whether or not some aspect of development is "normal." I think the most frequently asked questions are worth sharing because they may help you feel supported.

Frequently Asked Questions from Parents

Is it normal for my four-year-old to want to wear a princess costume when he plays at school and home?

Yes! That is totally normal. Playing dress-up is a normal part of child development and a fun way for children to interact, engage, and pretend. It can help them express themselves and their emotions in different ways and develop self-confidence (Coyne, Rogers, Shawcroft, and Hurst, 2021). And let's face it, playing dress-up is just good fun. The dramatic play area is a place where children can explore different roles, work together, and sort out problems. My students typically lean toward dressing up like movie characters or the current princess of the day. And often, children will explore less traditional gender roles. I have yet to find any research that would imply or support a negative outcome from boys wearing princess costumes or girls dressing up like cowboys.

Some children may begin to question gender at this age. Curiosity and exploration of gender is normal. Lindsay Rae Cohen, body image activist and mom, shared some insight with me on this topic in beautiful and inclusive way:

> As the parent of a nonbinary child, who I watched struggle to figure out who they are as a person, I have learned the monumental importance of letting a child explore gender roles in their own way. My beautiful

child explores the world around them with no boundaries and gets to decide who they are and who they want to be without any stigmatization on whether something should be male or female. The world is for them. There are no masculine or feminine roles but a world of possibilities without limitations. We have to teach our children the biology of their bodies so, as they age, they can advocate for their health. Forcing gender stereotypes is no longer the path forward. Let children explore the full gamut of human potential. Let boys play with dolls and girls play with cars and children in general explore and decide who they want to be without society's outdated forms of gender-expressive silos.

One of my favorite stories from my son Jack's childhood involves a story about playing dress-up. My husband came home to find our daughter, age five, and son, age three, playing dress-up in the playroom. My husband was upset to find his son in a Tinker Bell costume complete with a magic wand and wings. My husband said, "Jack, you need to go outside and play some football and get out of that dress!" Jack replied, "Hey, Dad! Bibbidi, bobbidi, boo!" and waived his fairy wand in his dad's general direction. My husband stormed off, angry at me for encouraging this type of play. But, my studies at Wheelock College and my graduate thesis were on this topic, so I knew Jack was going to be just fine.

Is it normal for my little girl not to be interested in "girl things?"

Yes, that's normal. Encourage children to explore all toys, games, and dramatic play. Labeling creates limitations in learning and development. When girls are encouraged to play with costumes, sing, dance, and play dress-up, this is fun. But, when we leave out building with blocks, designing, counting, creating, and experimenting, we do girls a disservice. Different parts of the brain are stimulated by different activities. To create well-balanced children who thrive in all areas and have the same chances to excel, it is essential to provide opportunities to learn based on equality, not gender. When girls are not encouraged to play with toys and experience opportunities to engage with science and spatial activities, it can affect their ability to develop relevant skills later in life. The same applies to boys. When boys are not encouraged to play in the dramatic play area or play with dolls, they may lose out on participating in nurturing and caregiving opportunities.

Even big toy brands such as Lego are trying to rid toys of gender bias: "Lego has announced it will work to remove gender stereotypes from its toys after a global survey the company commissioned found attitudes to play and future careers remain unequal and restrictive" (Russell, 2021). Further, the researchers found that while girls were becoming more confident and eager to participate in a wide range of activities, "71 percent of boys surveyed feared they would be made fun of if they played with what they described as 'girls' toys' —a fear shared by their parents" (Russell, 2021).

My son says he wants to be a girl one week and a boy the next. Is this normal?

Yes! Children explore their worlds and learn to play, pretend, and express themselves.

Many child development theorists and educators agree that play is an essential part of any early childhood education classroom setting.

Key characteristics of play, including uncertainty, challenge, and flexibility, influence "children's ability to adapt to, survive, thrive and shape their social and physical environments" (Lester and Russell, 2010). As children play, they tap into emotions, creativity, confidence, and self-expression. Play also gives children a time to experience disagreements and disappointments when other children don't share, get along with them, or understand how they are playing. Free play, when children get to play however they want with little guidance from adults, is always fun to observe. And you can learn so much about each child in this setting. The importance of children being able to play without intrusive adult controls or structure has been recognized as an important factor in promoting lifelong attributes, such as resilience and flexibility and the development and maintenance of children's social relationships (Mannello, Casey, and Atkinson, 2020). There is always a boy who wants to be Tinker Bell for the Halloween parade or a girl who dresses up like a cowboy in the dramatic play area. Some boys love to play in the classroom housekeeping area and dress up. Some girls love to play with blocks and trucks. Some children think they are dinosaurs, Harry Potter, Buzz Lightyear, or Snow White. Young children are full of imagination as they simultaneously develop thinking and social skills. They are learning to think, and their brains are changing, growing, and getting organized. Give them freedom to explore their environment, and allow them to play and explore without judgment.

Most boys know they are boys. Most girls know they are girls. Some children are not sure about their gender identity yet. Some children don't care about the labels and just play with everyone and try everything. Some boys have older sisters and copy everything their sisters do. Some girls have brothers and prefer to dress like their brothers. Assigning gender-based play restraints limits the potential of all children and feeds unhealthy stereotypes. Children need exposure and learning opportunities to play with all types of manipulatives and participate in all types of play to develop all parts of the brain.

If you would like to learn more about gender identity in young children, Guidance for Supporting Gender Diversity in Early Childhood Education by Jenny Fererro with Rebecca Bishop is a great resource.

My child goes to the bathroom frequently and has a rash around the genital area. Is this normal?

Frequent bathroom trips and rashes in private areas can be the result of a medical problem. Seek the help of a pediatrician. Children are typically in charge of cleaning and bathing themselves at this point. According to Stanford Children's Health Organization, "Incorrect wiping (child should wipe front to back) increases the risk of infections. This is even more risky after a bowel movement. Delaying going to the bathroom and constipation are also linked to urinary tract infections (UTIs)." Not to mention that germs spread like wildfire in preschool and kindergarten.

I had a kindergartener in my class who had started to smell, and he always had his hands in his pants scratching himself. The other students in my class referred to him as the smelly kid. I called the mom and found out that there was a new separation and the family was going through a divorce. The dad was not supervising the child's bath and reminding him to use soap and scrub with the washcloth. Was this sexual abuse? Absolutely not. But, the behavior was not normal for the child. I reached out because of a noticeable change in behavior and the smell. The dad emailed me to say that he was sorry and embarrassed and that he did not want his child to be labeled as a smelly kid.

Not every rash is automatically sexual abuse. But, anything related to irregularities with the private parts of the body may be a red flag that something is wrong. Also worth noticing are rashes around the lips and mouth. You can ask the child gentle questions if you cannot discern a medical cause or hygiene problem related to the irritation. For example, ask the child if anything has happened concerning their private parts. Has anybody inappropriately touched them? Parents and guardians, make sure to have the pediatrician check up on this situation to get an accurate diagnosis and report.

My child went on a playdate, and I found out the children played doctor. Is this normal?

It is normal for young children to be curious about each other's bodies. For children of the same age, this is not considered sexual abuse if the play is an isolated event and is innocent, consensual, and curiosity-based. If the children involved are of different ages, for example, a twelve-year-old and a kindergartner, or if a child is tricked, bribed, coerced, or forced to participate, then this behavior would not be appropriate.

A simple way to redirect this type of play is to review the body-safety rules with the child or with the children involved. Remind them that they can explore their own bodies in private. If they are curious about other people's bodies, they can ask Mom, Dad, or their trusted adult. Have welcoming, supportive communication on all things related to health and bodies. Include talking about the private parts, the names of these parts, and the rules related to these parts.

Frequently Asked Questions from Teachers

Is it normal for my students to always have their hands in their pants at school?

Yes. Children are curious creatures at this age and are exploring their bodies. It's normal for children to be curious about other bodies too. A kind, simple redirection is needed here; don't shame a child for this behavior.

If this becomes a habit and a distraction, reach out to the parents or guardians. Ideally, parents should use anatomically correct terms and talk with their children about privacy. Even though an action feels good, any self-exploration should be done privately, at home.

At naptime, one of my students lies on her stomach and bounces up and down with her hands in her pants. Is this normal?

Yes. It is pretty common for young children to masturbate occasionally in class at naptime (Leung and Robson, 1993). Some children may perceive that they have privacy because they may be under a blanket or they think everyone is sleeping. Others may do this because it is soothing and feels good.

I love the way Kathy Hakanson at Sex Ed Rescue, one of my go-to resources for comprehensive sex education, explains this tough topic for parents in her email to me on April 5, 2023.

> [Children] know that if they touch their genitals (or body) in a certain way, that a nice feeling will happen. And this feeling might help your child to fall asleep, to feel more relaxed, or just be something to do when they feel bored. This type of masturbation is different from adult masturbation . . . For adults, masturbation is when you might be touching yourself for sexual pleasure. . . Child masturbation is more about discovering that their genitals can feel nice when they touch them in a certain way.

You don't want to shame a child for doing something that feels good and is normal. A simple, kind, respectful redirection is all that is needed here: "Susan, can you please do that when you get home?" Teachers, I can't tell you how often I have seen preschool kids and kindergarteners exploring their private parts at nap time, on the playground, or in the bathroom. Most children this age are old enough to understand the concept of public versus private. They're also old enough to learn about body boundaries, rules, and consent. They need to learn early that no one—not even family members or other people they trust—should ever touch them in a way that feels uncomfortable or breaks a body-boundary rule.

They need to know that everybody's body is private. So, they should not touch or look at anyone else's private areas. In the classroom, a simple redirecting statement is key, but try to make this subtle and private. For example:

> TEACHER: Honey, I noticed you have your hands in your pants at naptime.

CHILD: I'm sorry.

TEACHER: Oh, I don't need you to apologize. You are not in trouble. You are the boss of your body. I just wanted to remind you that your private parts are private. So if you do that, you want to have privacy.

CHILD: What is privacy?

TEACHER: It just means a place that is at home and where you can be by yourself. Can you think of a place where you have privacy?

CHILD: My bedroom?

TEACHER: Yes! That is a private place.

CHILD: Why does that have to be private?

TEACHER: Because private parts have special rules. I will send home a note in your folder today with our body-safety rules, and you can talk about this more with your mom, okay?

CHILD: Okay. Thanks.

TEACHER: Do you have any other questions?

CHILD: No. I'm going to go play.

I have a student who refuses to wipe her bottom, and she is five. Is that normal?

That could be normal, depending on the situation. Some children are scared to go to the bathroom for fear of falling in the toilet. Some are scared to wipe their bottoms for fear of getting dirty. Some struggle with painful poops and get constipated quickly. Some children have pain when going to the bathroom. Those fears and feelings are normal for young children.

Try to encourage the child to wipe and try her best. Reach out to the parents to let them know what is happening at school. Ask yourself this: If this were my child, would I want to know? Yes!

I have a little boy in my class who has made sexual movements toward another student and used sexual language in the past month. This is a new behavior. Is this normal?

No, this is not normal. Any change in behavior that involves sexual gestures and sexual language is not typical for a young child. You will have to do some investigating. First, redirect the child.

Ask a few questions in a calm, gentle manner, for example, "Where did you learn that song (or that word)?" "What is that movement you are doing?" "Where did you learn that? Did you see a movie?" You don't want to make the child feel bad. They probably do not understand what they have seen or that it is wrong to reenact the gesture or language.

Call the parent or guardian and send a note home. Communicating this behavior with the parents and documenting the time, date, place, and other child involved is imperative. Let your director or principal know as well.

Is it normal for a relatively quiet child to suddenly have emotional outbursts and want to push, hit, and fight with any other children who get near him?

No, this is not normal. A sudden or even gradual change in behavior can be an indication of a problem brewing somewhere. C. Alexandria-Bernard Thomas, an abuse survivor, author, and advocate, shared the following in a telephone conversation with me on April 3, 2023 (shared here with their permission):

> I started acting out when I was being sexually abused by a friend of a family member. I was a normally quiet, passive kid. Almost overnight I started getting into fights all the time. I didn't want anybody to come near me. Had a teacher or other adult taken a minute to ask me, 'Hey, Chris, you have changed. You seem to be having some trouble handling emotions and fighting a lot. What is going on?' Then, maybe I would have been able to process what was going on and talk about it. And the look on my face coupled with silence is a sign. Changes in behavior, subtle and major, are signs. If only somebody gave me the safe space to talk. If only somebody asked me.

Is it normal for a preschool-age child to have an obsession with a binky and fight with any caregiver who would try to take it away?

Children can be overly attached to comfort items, such as pacifiers, blankets, and teddy bears.

A sudden, new obsession with a comfort item may be of concern. Ask the parent or guardian if there is any stress at home that would cause this new behavior. And ask the child why they feel they need the comfort item constantly.

> TEACHER: Mari, I noticed you just won't let go of your pacifier now. And we don't allow pacifiers at school. So, can we talk about what is happening?

> MARI: Okay. I like my pacifier because it reminds me of when I was a baby.

> TEACHER: How did you feel when you were a baby?

> MARI: Safe and cozy.

> TEACHER: Are you feeling safe and cozy at school?

> MARI: No! Not anymore.

> TEACHER: Why? You can tell me. I am a safe adult. I am here to help.

> MARI: He said not to tell you.

> TEACHER: You know that when somebody tells you to not tell or to keep a secret, I teach our class to always tell.

> MARI: Okay. You promise to help?

> TEACHER: Yes.

> MARI: Sam is being mean to me, and he broke the rules about private parts.

> TEACHER: Thank you for telling me. I believe you. I will speak with Sam and make sure you are safe. I am so proud of you for telling me.

MARI: Can I keep my pacifier? Should we call my mom?

TEACHER: That is a great idea. We will figure out how to make this class feel safe, and I will handle Sam.

MARI: Is Sam in trouble?

TEACHER: Mari, Sam made a big mistake. What we have to worry about is that you are safe.

MARI: Can we call my mom?

TEACHER: Yes, let's call your mom.

Is it normal for a kindergartener to have frequent, violent temper tantrums?

No, it is not normal for a kindergartener to have frequent, violent temper tantrums. This could be an indication that there is something going on with the child's overall health. This could also be a sign or symptom that the child is not able to handle emotions, is abused, or may be under some other duress that we don't know about. Reach out to the family, your school therapist, and your principal, and help find support for this child. Any changes in behavior must be noted. If you suspect child abuse in any way, remember that as a responsible adult you are a mandated reporter.

Frequently Asked Questions from Children

Endless questions from children are typical. Preschoolers and kindergarteners are full of often hilarious questions. When you get questions like these, try to answer directly and straightforwardly, focusing on the facts in an age-appropriate way. Being truthful encourages children to come to you with their questions in the future. You don't have to elaborate and go into graphic details. For example:

CHILD: Where do babies come from?

An appropriate answer might be, "When a mom and dad make a baby, it grows inside the mom's uterus. A uterus is part of a woman's body." Avoid the "stork" concept. That is just too confusing for a young child.

CHILD: Why doesn't my sister have a penis?

That is a great question! Boys and girls have different parts. Let's read this book to learn about our body parts.

CHILD: Why does my penis stand up?

A penis is part of your body and does many things. Let's talk about the things our bodies can do!

Your penis might stand up because you have to use the bathroom. Your penis might stand up if you play with it. It might stand up when you are sleeping. Sometimes, it can happen for no reason. That is all okay and just something your penis does. It's normal and happens to little kids and big kids.

Teaching Healthy Body Boundaries

Parents and guardians should begin to teach their children about body safety between the ages of two and five. Bathing and potty training are perfect opportunities to introduce conversations about parts of the body and consent. A great place to start is by introducing the anatomically correct names for children's body parts. Teaching children proper names for all body parts helps them in two ways. It shows any potential abuser that they know at least a little bit about body safety. It also helps a child report to an adult without any confusion over terms.

Talk about modesty. Teaching our children about modesty is a gentle way to introduce the concept of privacy and rules. We don't want children feel any shame about their bodies. We want them to be confident and secure in who they are and to love and respect their bodies. We also want them to understand that their naked bodies are meant to be private and only for them to see. By the time children are in kindergarten, they should know to keep their clothes on at school because school would be an inappropriate place to be naked and we have to keep our private parts private.

Teach consent. Parents and guardians, it is easy to introduce the concept of consent by modeling consent at home. Ask your child if they need help cleaning their body. Ask your child if you can have a hug. These are the beginnings of body autonomy, when children learn that they are the bosses of their bodies and have the right to say no to unwanted touch. Model consent with your partner frequently. For example, "Honey, I'm home! Can I please have a hug?"

"Yes? Thank you! Hug time."

"No? Okay, I will ask you later. How about a high five?"

Create body-safety rules for your family and review them frequently. Make sure to create a no-secrets rule for your family and explain why secrets can be dangerous. Clarify the difference between a secret and a surprise. Keep talking about body safety as your children grow. The topics will change organically. Encourage questions and conversation on the topic of body safety and sex education. Talk with your child's pediatrician and let them know that you are teaching your child about body safety and prevention. Also, let your child's teacher know that your child is learning about body safety. Offer to share your knowledge with your friends, family, and community.

Children can be interested in pregnancy and birth, especially if they are going to be a big sister or big brother. That is the perfect time to teach your children more about the female body, the male body, body terminology, and how babies are made. Keep your explanations simple and age appropriate.

Children this age might mimic dating, holding hands, fake kissing, and even weddings. Use these times as teachable moments, and don't be upset. Introduce age-appropriate topics such as suggesting that these friends head on over to the water table to play or try painting on the easel. Focus on supporting them and giving them boundaries without shame. Review body boundaries and private part rules (American Academy of Pediatrics, 2019). The Healthy Children website offers information on what is and isn't normal behavior in young children: https://bit.ly/4472vFS

Beyond dramatic play, sexual behavior problems in young children include any act that:

- **occurs way too much.** For instance, a child masturbating daily at nap time and in public, to the point where redirection is not working or the child has irritation and redness in the area.

- **can't be redirected.** For example, a child constantly touching themselves and trying to touch others in private areas, despite your redirection.

- **involves obscene language.** For example, the child uses words that you might hear from teens that describe sex acts, explicit sexual phrases, or words you might hear on a pornographic video. Calmly say, "Honey, I noticed that you are saying some adult words about sex. Where did you hear this? Do you want to talk about sex, or do you have any questions?"

- **is aggressive in nature.** For example, if a child were to kiss a friend and then hold them down with force or make sexual movements.

- **involves coercion or forceful phrases, such as bribes and threats.** For instance, if a child says, "I will be your best friend if you do something for me. If you don't do that for me, I won't be your friend," or "If you don't do that for me, I will tell all the kids at school what you did."

  For example, at a sleepover, a friend might say, "I will be your best friend if you touch my penis. All kids play doctor and touch each other. It's just fun," and then go on to say something like, "If you don't, I will tell all our friends that you touched my penis! So, you might as well do it anyway. Nobody will believe you because I have more friends than you." A child might also add bribery on top. For instance, a child might say, "I will give you fifty bucks if you show me your penis."

- **imitates adult sexual acts or gestures.** The child may have seen a YouTube video, clicked on a pop-up, or played a video game that has characters who simulate sex acts. Young children can be exposed to this type of content on the video games such as Roblox or on shows such as *Battle Kitty*.

Whenever you notice something different in behavior, pay attention. If you notice new words and gestures or play that is sexual in nature, ask questions. Try to approach the topic in a gentle tone of voice and avoid any confrontational language that may cause shame. Once you start having an open conversation in a nonjudgmental way, you can try to sort through where the child is getting these new phrases and ideas. You can remind the child of the body-safety rules and check in frequently to make sure these phrases and behaviors have stopped. Sometimes, the use of age-inappropriate language and phrases can be a sign of sexual abuse, but it can also be a sign that children are watching things online or on TV that they don't understand. Always remind the child when you have this type of a discussion that it is not their fault and that they can tell you anything and you will help, support, and love them—no matter what.

Your acceptance and willingness to answer all questions will provide a safe place to land. Your help and support will foster healthy attitudes and a sense of self-acceptance in your child. They will know they are always welcome to come to you with questions. You will become a trusted resource for your child. As parents or guardians of young children, teaching your child about their body and the functions of its parts is essential in developing healthy and safe habits.

Chapter 6

Creating Safe Spaces

Through the years, I have learned a few critical tips to help keep classrooms, homes, and spaces where children play a little safer. Ideally, we put together all of the prevention strategies we have just discussed and think about how to make every space as safe as possible. Most of these safe classroom strategies can apply to all circumstances, including monitoring children at home, at sports, and at all other activities.

Safer Classrooms

LINE OF SIGHT

Educators want to keep our classrooms as safe as possible. But, sometimes our cute ideas about decorating, dividing spaces, providing quiet book nooks, and places for the children to relax become part of the problem. It is important to keep the line of sight open. This means making sure that no areas are blocked from observation. One way teachers often go wrong is by having playhouses in the classroom or using large bookshelves as room dividers. A playhouse, such as one in the dramatic play center, can be a spot where it is hard to see what is going on inside. Playhouses on playgrounds are also an area of concern. You want to be able to see everyone, always. If you have a playhouse, I recommend removing it or removing the door and replacing it with a sheer piece of fabric.

Similarly, bookshelves and storage furniture can block line of sight. Consider pushing large pieces of furniture up against a wall to encourage open design and a clear field of vision. I do understand that some schools want classrooms to have a safe space to block an intruder from seeing the people the inside. Talk with your principal or director about classroom safety to decide what is best for your setting.

ATTENTION AND COMMUNICATION

Whenever you are supervising children, stay off your phone and keep your eyes on the children. Children can be so impulsive and silly! Walk around, and keep the children in your field of vision. And don't forget to do frequent head counts, or you might accidentally lose track of who is in the bathroom during your first-ever fire drill. (Yes! That was me on day three of my first kindergarten classroom.) If you have computers in your space, set them up in an open and observable area. Teach the children the rules for using the computers and review them frequently.

Consider setting up a red-flag mailbox. Cut out flag shapes from red paper and place them next to a decorated shoe box, along with a pen or pencil. Teach the children that if they have a body-boundary red flag, they can always tell you. But, if they are worried about telling you, they can put their name on a red flag and put it in the red-flag mailbox or simply hand it to you and you will talk to them right away.

THE RULE OF TWO

The rule of two—an adult should never be alone with a child. Sounds simple, doesn't it? It is one of the most basic sexual-abuse prevention practices you can institute at school. When an adult is alone with a child, there is an opportunity for abuse. To protect the children and yourself as a person who follows body-safety rules, try to keep this rule. There should never be one adult with one child under any circumstance other than a real emergency, for instance, if a child has an injury or other medical situation. We can run into problems with this rule in a school setting because, often, we need more staff to make this practical.

In a potty emergency, it is important to follow a strict procedure. An adult alone with a child in a bathroom can quickly turn into a misunderstanding with parents when the child gets home. Children can leave out details! Although you may have helped a child safely change clothes and guided them in cleaning up from a potty disaster, there is still room for a misunderstanding here. Consider that many children have trouble with potty disasters and need help unbuttoning their pants. Can you imagine a child getting home and telling their parent or guardian about a part of this situation?

> CHILD: Miss King unbuttoned my pants today.
>
> PARENT: What? Where? When?
>
> CHILD: When I was in the bathroom.
>
> PARENT: Was she helping you? What happened?
>
> CHILD (maybe embarrassed about the potty accident): I don't remember.

Next thing you know, you have a suspicious parent upset about a report from their little one.

Last year, I struggled with this rule. I taught at a small private school, and my kindergarten classroom was far away from the bathrooms. We scheduled trips to the bathroom four times each day: upon arrival, after snack, before lunch, and before recess. You would think that would be enough. (After all, as teachers, we often go through the whole day without even a five-minute break to hit the restroom for ourselves.) But a little student always tugs on my shirt and says, "Miss King, I have got to go to the bathroom bad!" My usual response is, "But we just went!"

Then the potty dance starts—you know, that dance when a child starts getting excited, jumpy, and holding on to their parts. So I have two options: Interrupt the whole class and take everyone to the bathroom again, or send the child to the bathroom with my teaching assistant. At our school, children cannot walk down the hallway alone without an adult. In a pinch, I typically send my assistant to escort the little person to the potty. But, this system leaves us open to problems. We're breaking our own rule out of necessity. However, there are ways to creatively work within this rule. Instead of the assistant going to the bathroom with one child, we decided to add an extra child or two. Adding a few students is not ideal, but it is the best we can do to keep the spirit of rule. Even though my assistant is alone with the children, she is not alone with one child.

We've always talked about how nice it would be to have a bathroom in the room. Ideally, that is the safest option, but you have to be careful with that situation as well. For example, you would never want two children in one bathroom at the same time because that presents an opportunity for body boundaries to be broken and is unsafe. Remember child-on-child abuse happens more often than we know. Children always need to be observable.

At the beginning of the school year, send a letter home explaining how you will safely handle this situation. Tell families that bathroom accidents are common at this age. Young children are still learning how to dress themselves and to recognize and respond to their bodies' signals about needing to use the bathroom. Explain how you will handle a potty accident, should it happen.

- Ask parents and guardians to send their child to school in clothing the child can put on and take off quickly.

- When there is an accident, tell them you will call home and let the parent or guardian know, and you will ask them to come to school with a change of clothes and wipes. The parent can get the child, clean them up, and bring them back.

Miss King's
CLASSROOM NEWSLETTER

UPCOMING EVENT

09/01/2023

Back-to-School Social

BODY SAFETY TIP

At home, practice having your child change their clothes. That way, if there is a mishap, your child will be able to handle this on their own. Being able to clean up and change clothes is an important skill.

THIS WEEK IN CLASS!

We can't wait to meet you at back-to-school night!

Please bring all of your signed paper-work, your summer packet, and an extra change of clothes for your child. The extra set of clothes is **in case your child has a bathroom accident at school**—which is common at this age.

During this first week, please send in a box of tissues, hand sanitizer, and wipes for the class.

REMINDERS:

- Bring your child's school supplies.
- Let's set up your child's locker and desk.
- Get ready for a fun year!

- If the parent or guardian cannot come to school, offer noncontact assistance. This means you will stand by the bathroom door and talk the child through what they need to do.

  ▸ Take off your dirty clothes.

  ▸ Put your dirty clothes in this bag.

  ▸ Use these wipes to clean up. Wipe front and back. Clean up twice.

  ▸ Put on clean underwear, fresh clothes, socks, and shoes.

  ▸ Wash your hands.

Even in the biggest potty disasters, it is best not to have direct contact with any private area. The parent and caretaker in you might want to jump in and help your poor little student with the poopy mess. But, my advice is to avoid doing this. Somebody might misunderstand or accuse you of something because you were alone with the child during this situation.

If you have the staff for a potty emergency, use two adults to witness, document, guide, and assist. And because helping involves possible contact with bodily fluids, use all hygiene and safety protocols here, including gloves.

HOW PARENTS AND GUARDIANS CAN HELP THEIR CHILDREN HANDLE POTTY EMERGENCIES

Prepare your children to know they will probably have at least one accident at school, so practice what to do if that happens.

> AUNTIE: I'm so excited! You are such a big boy and are going to school this year. It is going to be so much fun. But what would you do if you had a potty emergency?

> THOMAS: What's a potty emergency?

AUNTIE: You know, like an accidental poop or pee. Or you throw up, barf, vomit.

THOMAS: Wouldn't my teachers help me?

AUNTIE: Yes, they definitely would. But I want you to learn what to do to make it easier for you and them. Let's practice.

THOMAS: Okay, if you think it's a good idea.

AUNTIE: Let's give it a try. Imagine you are covered in throw-up all over everything. What would you do first?

THOMAS: Ask my teacher for help.

AUNTIE: Okay, and then what?

THOMAS: I don't know. I would probably be sad and gross.

AUNTIE: Let's make sure you can get off all your yucky clothes. Let's pretend I am the teacher. I will stand by the door and talk you through this. I will give you a plastic bag for your dirty clothes. I want you to take them off. I won't look. Okay?

THOMAS: Okay.

AUNTIE: So, Thomas, can you put all the yucky stuff in the big plastic bag? Then pass it to me.

THOMAS: Sure. Here you go. Now what?

AUNTIE: Take these wipes and clean up.

THOMAS: But I'm not dirty.

AUNTIE: I know. We're just practicing, remember?

THOMAS: Oh, right! Ha ha.

AUNTIE: Are you all clean?

THOMAS: Yes! Can I get some clean clothes around here?

AUNTIE: Okay, I am not coming in. I will leave this bag of clean clothes right by the door where you can reach them. You come to get them.

THOMAS: Alright.

Auntie waits a few minutes. Thomas is dressed.

AUNTIE: You did it. But we forgot one thing.

THOMAS: What?

AUNTIE: You need to wash your hands.

THOMAS: Oh yeah.

Thomas comes out of the bathroom.

AUNTIE: How was that?

THOMAS: Easy.

AUNTIE: So if this happens at school, you know you don't have to worry. You already know how to get rid of yucky clothes, clean up, and get back into clean clothes.

THOMAS: Yup.

AUNTIE: Great! High five. Did you need anybody to come in the bathroom with you?

THOMAS: Nope! I did it all by myself. But what if it is yucky and I'm still sick?

AUNTIE: Then your teacher will call me, and I will come to get you. I'll help you at home. You would probably shower, and I would tuck you into bed.

THOMAS: Okay. Thanks for practicing with me. I hope I don't puke at school!

AUNTIE: Me too! But if you do, now you know what to do. And guess what. Miss King told me that every year lots of children have a potty accident. So, it is normal.

Safer at Home

PLAYDATES AND SLEEPOVERS

When you have playdates at your own home, review the body-safety rules with your child before the friend arrives. Talk to the other parent or guardian before the playdate to express your body-safety education efforts. If the other parent or guardian is interested, share books on body safety with them.

Explain your body-safety rules to the visiting child. An easy way to have this conversation is to start the playdate with a safety check.

> MOM: Hey guys, before you go play can we review our body-safety rules?
>
> CHILDREN: Sure!
>
> MOM: Let's go over to the fridge and look at our rules. Can we read them together?
>
> CHILDREN: Okay, can you help us?
>
> MOM: Sure! (Mom and children do a choral reading of the posted rules.) Everybody understand?
>
> CHILDREN: Yes!
>
> MOM: Thumbs up?
>
> CHILDREN: Thumbs up!
>
> MOM: Okay. Remember to keep the doors open and call me if you need me. I will be up to check on you in a few minutes.

Another great way to introduce body safety to a new friend is to play the body safety songs "My Body My Rules" or "Da House Rules," available at https://youtube.com/playlist?list=PLzsG1mmBBF58_MbyeHsgVhl-U-gGvSAAc

Regardless of the setting, the following tips apply:

- Always supervise children in open areas where you can see them constantly.

- Check in frequently.

- If the children will be changing into bathing suits, have them do so separately and in private.

- Keep all children out of bedrooms.

- Keep all doors open to observe play.

- Make sure the children go to the bathroom separately.

When your child is having a playdate at a friend's house, the risk changes. No matter how well prepared your child is with body-safety strategies, you just don't know what goes on behind the closed doors of other families. If you are comfortable with playdates, I recommend staying at the playdate and chatting with the caregiver. Watch how the parent or guardian supervises and engages with the children. Notice whether the children are allowed in bedrooms, basements, or playrooms alone. Find out who else will be in the house. Are there older brothers or sisters, cousins, or neighbors? Ask a lot of questions in an attempt to try to find out what the rules are at this house.

If you feel comfortable with letting your child play there, make sure to review with the other parent or guardian that your child is learning about body safety. If your child says they want to go home or reports any problems, you expect to be called right away. Keep the first playdate short.

For sleepovers, do the same preparation that you do for playdates. Once, when my son was at a sleepover, we had a relatively normal "Let's play doctor" kind of event. My neighbor called me and said, "I just walked in on the kids playing doctor. They were using a stethoscope and being a little bit curious about each other's parts. I redirected the kids, and they went to play on the jungle gym outside. Everyone is okay, and we reviewed body-safety rules. Do you want to come over?" I headed over, and this mom and I chatted and discussed how important it is to do frequent check-ins on the children. Even when you are supervising carefully, little ones can slip away for a few minutes and end up playing doctor in the bathroom with their pants down.

When this activity is based in genuine curiosity on the part of both children and there is no coercion, no threats or tricks, and involves questions and looking, I tend to take these experiences as normal childhood curiosity and teachable moments. Children are curious creatures. If you have spent time around a two- or three-year-old, you have answered your fair share of questions: "Why? But, why?"

I don't recommend sleepovers for children younger than twelve, and then only with a friend of the same age. Even in your own home, it is too hard to adequately monitor the children unless you want to stay up all night. As my grandma use to say, "I never let my kids do sleepovers or have sleepovers because nothing good happens after 9:00 p.m." Grandma was wise and always right.

SIBLINGS

I hate to bring this up, but sibling sexual abuse (SSA) is more common than you might realize. Unfortunately, the topic is often considered taboo, so nobody really talks about it with their children. In a recent chat with my friend and fellow sexual-abuse prevention advocate Jane Epstein, she said, "Sibling sexual trauma is real. It happens in all types of families. In fact, it is one of the most common forms of child sexual abuse both in the US and worldwide."

Part of prevention is awareness and body-safety education. This is a great resource where you can find more information: https://www.siblingsexualtrauma.com/

- **Keep doors open when children are playing together.** When you keep the doors open in rooms, children are observable. Abuse happens when children are unsupervised or unobservable. Some families have gone the extra mile to install cameras or nanny cameras in the house to monitor children.

- **When possible, keep siblings in their own rooms and beds.** Ideally, each child should have their own bed and room, but this is not practical for many families. I shared a room with my sister Kathy, and we divided the room with an imaginary line. Our mom was strict about privacy and respect. Kathy slept in her bed on her side, and I slept on mine. When we played in our room, the door was open and we were observable.

- **Talk about privacy and body safety constantly.** Introducing body safety, boundaries, and rules is critical to keeping siblings safe. Create an environment where telling is encouraged. If a sibling breaks a body-boundary rule or refuses to respect someone's space or comfort level, it is always okay to tell a safe adult.

- **Review consent.** In our email exchange on March 3, 2023, Rosalia Rivera of Consent Parenting said, "Consent is the permission someone should ask for before doing something to or with you, like a hug, a kiss, a tickle. They should ask you first, and you get to say yes or no to their request." This advice applies to personal space in shared bedrooms as well. When siblings live in shared rooms, developing boundaries within the room can help everyone. If there are two sisters living in the same room and sleeping in separate beds, a conversation about the beds being part of a boundary might be a good idea. For instance, the bed on the right is Kathy's bed. The bed on the left is Kimmy's bed. These beds are private spaces for each of you. Your sister would need to ask if she can some sit with you on your bed, and you would need to respectful of her personal space and ask her if you can sit on her bed.

- **Communication is critical.** If your children know that body boundaries and consent are a part of your family's rules and they feel comfortable telling you when there are problems, you have an opportunity to reduce the risk of sibling sexual abuse. Remember that it is okay to ask your child, "Has your brother ever made you feel unsafe or uncomfortable?" or "Has your sister ever touched your private parts?" Stress that being part of a safe family means that we all learn about safety and let the safe adults know when there are problems so we can talk about the problems and fix them.

Take a minute to write down your experiences. Ask your children if they have had any negative, red-flag experiences in any spaces at school, at home, or anywhere else.

We all have at least one embarrassing moment or uncomfortable memory in our memory banks. Sharing your experiences with your children might help them feel more supported and might help them open up. I hope that your memory and these questions have not triggered anything too serious. If they have, I encourage you to write more about it. Or, consider calling a friend or therapist to talk about it. Sometimes repressed childhood memories bubble up when we are talking about this topic. When you are ready, let's move from looking at problems to and taking action toward prevention. In the next section, my colleague John-Michael Lander and I offer some advice on sexual-abuse prevention in children's activities.

Safer Sports and Activities

Most children join in some form of organized physical activity, sport, club, or lessons. Maybe your preschooler is a soccer player or loves T-ball. Perhaps you have a twirling ballerina, a vocalist, or an aspiring gymnast in the family. Or maybe you have a young Cub Scout, Webelo, Daisy, or Brownie. Roles that give adults access to children, such as coaching or club leadership, can be attractive to sexual predators. Proactive sexual-abuse prevention and body-safety skills before participating in activities will help protect the entire family from sexual abuse. Asking questions related to safety to these groups will also help protect children:

- Do these groups screen and conduct background checks on leaders?

- Do they have sexual-abuse prevention training?

- Do they follow sexual-abuse prevention strategies and have a system in place to keep children monitored at all times?

- Do they have a prevention policy?

From our organizations at the Darkness to Light National Prevention Conference, Ignite 2019, I learned just how essential it is to demand sexual-abuse prevention policies. At this conference, I heard Aly Raisman, Olympic gymnast and survivor, speak in person and share her story. In addition to her athletic accolades, you may recognize her as one of the girls and young women who were sexually abused by a former Team USA doctor. As she spoke, one thing that really struck me was her statement, "I didn't know the signs. I didn't know what sexual abuse really was. And I think that needs to be communicated to all of these athletes, no matter the age."

A great deal of sexual abuse can be prevented when we empower children, families, and members of organizations with facts and help them learn the signs of grooming and tools to prevent child sexual abuse.

Abuse occurs in all types of sports and activities. I have always trusted the coaches our family has trained with—but not blindly, because of my background. I have respect for the people who volunteer their time and effort to contribute to the community through youth clubs and sports. But, some adults who volunteer in these organizations do so simply because they know there is access, time, opportunity, and trust from the families, participants, and organizations.

In 2020, the US Center for SafeSport surveyed four thousand athletes across fifty sports. The survey found that 40 to 50 percent of athletes have experienced mild to severe harassment or abuse (US Center for Safesport, 2022). As a parent, teacher, or school administrator, I encourage you to check out the US Center for SafeSport. This organization maintains a database and connects the public to ongoing investigations related to misconduct, sexual abuse, abuse, and harassment by coaches.

PREVENTIVE ACTIONS AND POLICIES

Parents and guardians must get the pulse on the environment and attitudes regarding safety at their children's sports teams and clubs from the start. A proactive prevention and safety policy should include a mandatory meeting for all parents and guardians, coaches and leaders, support staff, and participants to address acceptable behavior. Safety precautions should include the rule of two: no adult will be alone with one child. This rule protects children from physical and sexual abuse. This is also a commonsense rule to protect leaders and coaches in the rare event of a false report. The organization should have a written policy for reporting concerns, issues, and abuse that is clear and easy for families and children to follow.

What does a healthy sexual-abuse prevention climate look like?

- The organization trains leaders, coaches, and all support staff in sexual-abuse prevention.

- Leaders, coaches, and support staff are vetted annually.

- The sexual-abuse prevention policy, with rules and consequences that protect children, is shared with families.

- The organization has a tradition of safety, not initiations and hazing. Anti-hazing and anti-bullying programs are implemented with all participants, and policies are strictly enforced.

- The organization has a culture of respect for all genders and sexual orientations.

- Coaches, leaders, and staff respond immediately to all incidents and reports that occur.

- The practices, lessons, and/or meetings have an open-door policy for parents and guardians.

- Leaders and coaches closely monitor all children under their supervision.

- Mixing different age groups is not allowed in locker rooms, bathrooms, campsites, and so on.

- The organization leaders, coaches, and support staff observe a healthy balance between respecting a child's need for privacy when they change clothing and ensuring the safety of every child.

Parents and guardians should explain to their children that it is always okay to tell. If they see something wrong or unsafe, they should tell somebody. Remind children that you are 100 percent open and ready to talk. It is never too late to tell, and you will help them, even if they make a mistake.

John-Michael Lander, founder of An Athlete's Silence (https://anathletessilence.com/), gave a presentation at the Coalition to End Sexual Exploitation 2022 Online Global Summit. We connected afterward because his story and organization were really eye-opening for me. His message about organizational and sport-related grooming is one that every parent or guardian needs to know before they involve their children in any sport or organization. When we talked, Lander shared his thoughts on prevention and creating safe environments and safer sports.

The locker room is minimally supervised by adults. [It's a place] where uninterrupted small talk occurs and vulnerability is high. This free time can escalate into many forms of abuse, fights, bullying, intimidation, and sexual exploitation.

[P]arent awareness is critical here for safety and prevention. The predators first groom the institution, the parents, and eventually the athlete. Nobody knows this! Just the knowledge of this system is empowering. It is something we can and must look out for to prevent situations like the US Gymnastics Federation scandal.

Taking an active and preventative stance in early childhood can change things for your child and all children. Talk and listen to your children. An abused child wants to be heard and believed. An abused child is shameful and embarrassed and may be reluctant to come to a parent or guardian. It is the adult's role to notice any changes that could be questionable. Parents, guardians, and caring adults can work together to make an incredible, life-saving impact as children are empowered. Lander recommends the following steps for parents, guardians, and organizations to work together to keep kids safe:

- At the start of the school-year activities and each sports season, begin conversations with parents and guardians, coaches, leaders, and support staff. Emphasize behaviors that will not be tolerated. During this opening talk, discuss with the adults what to look for in children's behavior and how to report any concerns or behavior issues. Put a policy in place to protect a person who reports, to prevent retaliation, revenge, or intimidation.

- With the children, discuss the behavior expectations and the importance of being an active bystander who tells an adult when they see a problem. Put a policy in place to protect a child who reports, to prevent retaliation, revenge, or intimidation.

Work for a body-safe community by including parents, teachers, administrators, coaches, and all staff to improve safe hiring practices and sexual-abuse prevention policies. Teaching children how to respect themselves, each other, the rules, and the boundaries is a critical part of childhood and needed in all environments. What if we could shift the thinking here and empower children to understand and respect body autonomy and consent in preschool? These strategies have the potential of creating a real change and protecting children from harm in the future. Eventually, children will be in places where their parents or guardians are not present. Children are not responsible for protecting themselves, but they do need to know about the body, boundaries, and consent. They need to be able to identify when they are in danger and how to use an assertive voice and a safety plan. (We explore these topics in detail in later chapters.)

✗ ✗ ✗

We as adults must consider our own choices, too. We are the first line of defense against any predator. Are we being as safe as possible when we choose our child's karate class, dance instructor, or child care? Are we doing things online that put our children in danger? In the next chapter, we will consider online risks and mistakes that many parents have made (myself included). Keep reading because you will learn about behaviors that you might be doing that put the whole family at risk. The good news is you can fix most of these online safety risks quickly and avert danger.

Chapter 7

Don't Post That! Online Safety

Teachers, parents, and guardians need to work together and start early to prepare children with the facts and information about risks. Empathetic, clear, supportive conversations are key to home and school online safety. When we are aware of these possible risks, we can educate and empower children with support and safety tools from safe adults. If they ever make a mistake, children will know that they have a support system of responsible adults working with them in a nonjudgmental way. The good news is that many incredible people are working hard to keep children safe. And the more you know, the safer children are.

Early childhood is a period in which children reach crucial developmental milestones. Positive and negative influences may promote or inhibit this sensitive process (Madigan et al., 2019). Among these influencing factors, media exposure can have an effect on early childhood development (Michaelis and Niemann, 2004). Studies have shown that greater levels of screen time are associated with poorer physical health and obesity in later life (Hancox, Milne, and Poulton, 2004). School-aged children and adolescents with moderate or high levels of exposure to media were found to have lower psychological well-being (Twenge and Campbell, 2018). Studies have demonstrated that high media use by preschool-aged children is related to conduct problems, hyperactivity, and inattention later in life (Poulain et al., 2018).

Common Sense Media conducted surveys in 2015 and 2021 on children's cellphone and social media use. The research and advocacy organization found that the proportion of eight-, nine-, and ten-year-olds with their own smartphones nearly doubled in those years (Rideout, 2016; Rideout, Peebles, Mann, and Robb, 2021).

Even young children can take pictures of themselves and friends with a click. My nephew Briggs loves to take videos with his parents' phones. Whenever I come over to babysit, he asks me to take a video of him launching his paper airplane, and he always requests slow motion. I love the look of joy that my nephew gets when he watches himself launch that old-fashioned airplane in the sky with a simple twist of a rubber band and a toss. Supervised cellphone use can be really fun and entertaining, but there is so much more that makes them just awful for young children.

Most three- to eight-year-olds are not operating their own social media accounts, but some are! Five-year-olds who attended online school during the COVID-19 pandemic know how to navigate Zoom with ease. (Most of my students knew how to operate Zoom better than I did.)

Take a minute to think about the content your children are absorbing through media and how it may carry over into physical spaces and create unsafe situations. For example, *Battle Kitty* from Netflix includes sexual references and gestures. If your child happened to see some of the sexual gestures in this cartoon, they may try to put objects in others' underpants. Cartoons, YouTube, video games—these media are unsafe without parental supervision and heavy monitoring. As a teacher, I have seen children recreate the things they have seen on TV and online over and over again. I often feel that some shows and online games are grooming our children in an invisible way.

Current Online Safety Issues

We can't deny the incredible influence of the online world. A study by the Pew Research Center showed that 80 percent of children between the ages of five and eight have access to tablets, and 53 percent of children in that age group use cellphones. Further, the statistics for children under age five reveals that 48 percent use tablets and 55 percent use cellphones (Auxier, Anderson, Perrin, and Turner, 2020). Technology offers many benefits when it comes to both learning and entertainment, but the ease with which young children can access pornography on digital devices is deeply troubling—and damaging their development.

Cybersafety is a critical issue for families, schools, and children. As a sexual-abuse prevention advocate, I spend a great deal of time explaining to parents and guardians that the risk for children regarding sexual abuse lies within the inner circle of people they already know.

But, I believe that statistics are changing because of the online risk.

In 2020, the COVID-19 pandemic brought an already dangerous online situation to a new level. Predators who spend time on the dark web and usually hang out in chat rooms where they do not have to register, such as the Omegle platform, have moved to where our children hang out online.

My friend and online-safety expert Kristen A. Jenson, author of *Good Pictures, Bad Pictures: Porn-Proofing Today's Young Kids* and *Good Pictures Bad Pictures Jr.: A Simple Plan to Protect Young Minds*, offers this advice: "Keeping kids safe from sexual abuse must include teaching them to recognize, reject, and report pornography exposure. Predators use porn as an effective grooming tool to normalize child sexual behavior and reduce a child's inhibitions, as well as to teach kids what the perpetrator wants them to do. Additionally, kids who innocently view pornography may end up imitating that behavior on younger, more vulnerable children. For kids to be safe from hands-on sexual abuse, they must learn to reject pornography, which acts as a form of sexual abuse when children view it."

Predators are on YouTube, Instagram, Xbox, Roblox, TikTok, Facebook, and Snapchat, among others. Online grooming happens everywhere, right under our noses, as children play video games or chill on their phones. Technology changes so fast that many parents and teachers are overwhelmed by the mountains of information and danger. We must overcome our fears and learn about these constant and increasing risks. While there is no way to become an expert on all the risks, we can make a dent in protecting children with education and communication in a judgment-free zone.

Online Safety Tips for Parents and Guardians

First, let's assess where you are in the social media situation. If you are a parent or guardian, take a minute to write down your children's access to technology at school and home, what technology they use, and what limits they have. Also, write down what safety apps or software you have. Obviously most preschoolers through third graders don't have their own cellphones, but often they do have access to them through older siblings and parents or guardians, and most children use technology at school daily. So, it is important to understand where the risks are and how to get ahead of them. Charlene Doak-Gebauer, author of *The Internet: Are Children in Charge? Theory of Digital Supervision* (2019), advises that the best way to keep children safe from the online risk is to avoid buying them a cellphone and to keep them away from other devices. But, she suggests that once they do have access to devices, parents and guardians should apply digital supervision. For example, she suggests that parents and children discuss and agree on a contract to establish rules of online behavior. Surprisingly, children may come up with rules that will be a part of the contract.

Basic digital safety practices include the following:

- Do not allow your child to have a computer, cellphone, or tablet in their bedroom.

- Parents or guardians must have the passwords for all devices.

- Cellphones and tablets must be docked in the adults' bedroom at night for charging.

- Teach children that they should never take their clothes off for anybody online, even if the person in the chat sends them threatening messages. They must tell a safe adult and know that they will not get in trouble.

Parents and guardians can monitor children's cellphone and tablet use the old-fashioned way by communicating and being present when children use these devices. You can also look at any chats and text, read the emails, and look at the photos and deleted images.

You also may want to consider parental monitoring and controls. This can be a tricky topic once children are old enough to understand what this means. In my opinion, it is essential to monitor your young children online until you have developed enough trust and a safety plan that is comprehensive and based on communication, educa-tion, support, and love in a nonjudgmental zone. Children are going to make mistakes. They live in a world where expressing emotions and needs and—later—even sexuality online is commonplace. They need to learn how to be safe and intuitive before they participate. We need to give them the space to make mistakes without fear of judgment or embarrassment.

PARENTAL MONITORING APPS

Apps such as Bark Technology alert parents and guardians to certain content topics, bullying language, suicidal talk, self-harm, abuse, sexual abuse, and abusive language. The app lets you know that there is a situation going on.

Positives:

This helps parents get ahead of problems and ask questions.

It provides a safety net.

It keeps online safety as a topic of active discussion and evaluation.

The app has the ability to monitor multiple devices at one time and send your coordinates alerts.

Bark can block certain inappropriate images.

You can adjust settings to give your child less or more privacy based on their age.

Negatives:

If your child is being monitored, they may take extra steps to get around it.

They may resent you for not trusting them.

They may feel that you are violating their privacy.

They may feel entitled to have private conversations with friends.

They may use other kids' phones to communicate things they are trying to hide.

They may get more sneaky and not feel comfortable telling you what is really going on.

They may buy a burner phone and keep you out of that loop.

Despite the negatives, parental controls or parent monitoring are something I recommend. But, more important than the controls and monitoring is developing communication around body safety. Talking openly, honestly, and frequently about body safety—both on- and offline—is the most important thing you can do for your children. When a child feels safe, loved, and supported to know that if they make a mistake they can come to you with no judgment, they will come to you. When they are faced with a problem that is too big for them to handle, you want them to trust you to keep them safe.

Keep in mind that, even if you do prepare your children, it is not fair, realistic, or responsible to think that young children will be able to handle an aggressive predator who has been grooming them. This is why your cyber IQ is essential. You have to know the risks and get ahead of them as best you can with parental controls, safety apps, monitoring, reading, research, and talking. Keeping this communication open, honest, helpful, and supportive will enable your children to come to you when they need help. These conversations are so important and save lives.

- **Talk about it:** Sit down and talk about the dangers of online content. Children need to know that the internet is not designed for kids. If they come across scary or inappropriate content, they need to look away, leave the device, and tell a safe adult. Keep your conversations on digital safety open, honest, supportive, and nonjudgmental.

- **Ask:** Ask children if they have seen anything online or if a friend has shown them anything online that made them feel unsafe or uncomfortable. If so, that is a red flag.

- **Supervise:** Do not let children under the age of twelve go online unsupervised. If your children have to be online, sit with them and monitor what they do.

- **Set time limits:** Keep online time to a minimum. Instead, connect face-to-face. Put devices to bed! Lock them up every night in the adults' bedroom. Establish rules and boundaries for devices and time spent online.

- **Check the device history and add parental controls:** While nothing is foolproof, many apps are available that can help guide parents to improve safety. I recommend Bark Technologies and Gabb Phone.

- **Communicate online safety rules clearly:** Consider creating a family online safety contract, such as the following on page 92. Go over it and sign it with your child. Post it where you all can see it, and review it frequently.

Family Online Safety Contract

Kids

- ☐ I will respect myself online.

- ☐ I will not share my name, my parents'/guardians' names, my address, my town, my phone number, or my school name with anybody.

- ☐ I will not take photos or videos of my body parts.

- ☐ I will not send photos or videos to anybody.

- ☐ I will tell if anybody sends me photos or videos.

- ☐ I will tell if I have a problem with anybody on any topic online.

- ☐ I will always get help from a safe adult. My safe adults are

  _____.

Parents or Guardians

- ☐ We will have open, honest communication.

- ☐ You can tell us anything.

- ☐ We will listen and help without judgment.

- ☐ We expect that mistakes will happen.

- ☐ Your safety is our first concern.

Sign and Date _____

Sign and Date _____

Have conversations with your children about the dangers of sharing photos online. Check in with your child frequently to discuss this topic, and ask if anybody has ever asked them to send a picture on a device. Share that you will support them and help them no matter what!

Remember, children cannot give consent. A person who pressures a child to send nude photos should be held responsible for the coercion and manipulation involved in acquiring such content. Once such a person has an image, they are engaging with child sexual-abuse material. Sending sexually explicit texts, called sexting, to a minor is legally classified as child sexual abuse. These are federal crimes in the United States. If a child is being exploited, contact your local FBI field office, call 1-800-CALL-FBI, or report it online at https://tips.fbi.gov

THE DANGERS OF POSTING PHOTOS ON SOCIAL MEDIA

I know, I know . . . Your baby's bath time is adorable, and you want to share that cuteness with the world. Your child is too young to know the dangers of posting photos online. Even though you might think it is cute and fun, it can be hazardous. There are sick individuals out there searching Instagram right now for a photo of your baby's butt! Your child can't consent to photo sharing. These pictures will live forever in digital space, and you can't take that back. If you knew what pedophiles do with your photos, you would be sick to your stomach and never post a picture of your child again.

- Do not post naked or partially naked photos.

- Do not post your child's face online.

- Do not take pictures with identifying clothing, such as a school name, or your location settings on.

- Tell your family and friends not to post photos of your children without your permission.

- If you have to post pictures, refrain from using hashtags.

- Use apps and services such as Honeycomb or Shutterfly to share within the family by invitation only.

When you add a hashtag, you make it easy for a pedophile to find your photos. The Child Rescue Coalition (2023) warns, "Most parents post 1,500 photos of their child before they turn five. While this might seem cute and innocent and increases 'likes,' it can overexpose children by showcasing private moments they might not like to be shared with a large audience, making them vulnerable to pedophiles and sex offenders. Parents often include hashtags without understanding how predators use these to search for our kids."

Using hashtags, child molesters, predators, and pedophiles search for free images to use, collect, and share. If you have to post pictures, refrain from using hashtags at all. (The Child Rescue Coalition website offers a list of particular hashtags to avoid.)

I did a little research on this by searching some hashtags in the search bar on Instagram. I searched #Nakedtoddler, and sure enough, more than one thousand images of naked toddlers popped up. I chose two similar photos of naked toddlers, and I compared the information:

- Both moms posted naked pictures of their toddlers.

- Both moms had open accounts that were not set to private. Anybody could see these photos.

- Both moms had stories about their cute toddlers and how they loved being naked.

- Both moms had lots of friends commenting on the naked pictures.

- These moms don't follow each other.

Both moms had one mysterious follower in common who liked their pics. When I searched for that person's online name, BigDaddyD1982, I found that the account has many red flags.

- The account has a slogan about cancer, instead of a photo, as a profile pic.

- The account is set to private.

- The account has twenty-six followers.

- The followers have suspicious-looking accounts too.

- The account follows twenty-seven other accounts, most of moms and children.

- BigDaddyD1982 has commented on a ten-year-old's account on Instagram.

Oh, wait! You thought you had to be thirteen years old to be on Instagram, and they check your age with verification? Um, no. Each platform offers ways that a predator can exploit to access children, gather information, groom, and trick you and your children.

And it gets worse. Now there are apps available that can easily change a predator's face from a fifty-five-year-old male to that of a young girl in a minute. Predators can also use deepfake software to manipulate your child's face and put it on a different person's body in a photo or video. They can then use these images to manipulate, blackmail, and extort your family. Sextortion is rising, and the Federal Bureau of Investigation (FBI) and The National Center on Sexual Exploitation (NCOSE) are ringing the alarms.

Sextortion is a cybercrime in which predators claim to have or actually have an image of the target and threaten to expose the picture to family, friends, and a child's school unless the family pays a ransom. According to the FBI, "Sextortion can start on any site, app, messaging platform, or game where people meet and communicate. Sometimes, the first contact with the criminal will be a threat. The person may claim to have already a revealing picture or video of a child that will be shared if the victim does not send more pictures. More often, however, this crime starts when young people believe they are communicating with someone their own age who is interested in a relationship or with someone who is offering something of value" (FBI, n.d.).

Often, criminals will threaten to publish a photo or video or threaten violence to get the victim to produce more images, or they will demand money or gift cards. The shame, fear, and confusion children feel when they are caught in this cycle can prevent them from asking for help or reporting the abuse. Families and caregivers should understand how this crime occurs and openly discuss online safety with children. I know this is scary! But, this is one area where your knowledge of online sexual exploitation can keep your children safe.

THE DANGER OF APPS

When you do decide to allow your children to have cellphones and access to other devices, it's time to learn about the latest apps and technology. Safety settings change and new apps are developed daily, so it is important to keep up. The following list isn't arranged in order of most dangerous to least dangerous. Each app or platform has different features with varying levels of inappropriateness.

- **Snapchat:** Snapchat allows users to post and share photos and videos. It has the dangerous and misleading feature of "disappearing messages." When a user posts a photo or video message, that content is available for only a short time before it is no longer accessible. However, most children don't understand that a person who receives a video or photo can take a screenshot before the message disappears. This puts children at risk of sextortion. The most disturbing part of this app is the Snap Map, which shows exactly where a user is located. Strangers who pose as friends can have GPS directions to where your child is. If you choose to allow your child to use Snapchat, insist that they always have their account set to "private," they always turn off their location, and they only accept friend requests from people you know personally and can verify.

- **Instagram:** There is quite a lot of adult content on Instagram. Even if your child's account is private, your child is still at risk for viewing pornography and other adult content. All your child needs to do is a quick search based on a hashtag and there it is! Your child's private account does not keep them from viewing anybody else's account. Instagram also has a disappearing message button. If you choose to allow your child access to Instagram, insist that they always have their account set to private, they always turn off their location, and they only accept friend requests from people you know personally and can verify. Instagram has created something called Family Center to help parents monitor what their child sees. According Instagram, "Family Center is a place where parents can view the accounts they supervise on Instagram and manage super-vision settings" (Meta, 2023).

- **Discord:** This is a massive space for teens to chat and talk about gaming and other, often adult, topics. It's a messaging platform that features chatrooms, direct messaging, voice chat, and video calls. Because of this, it is hard to monitor. "Users can join different 'servers' that are like themed chat rooms that feature text, voice, and video chat. Servers can revolve around any topic—from huge public servers . . . to small, private groups of friends" (Bark, 2021). This tricky app can expose children to a huge assortment of terrible content, including bullies, porn, and sexual predators. Discord is used by more than just young people playing video games. It is a bit of a cesspool for adult content. It is easy for children to make "friends" with adults who may be up to no good.

- **Yik Yak:** Yik Yak is an anonymous chat app that lets children engage with other users within a radius from their phone. This is super dangerous! I do not recommend allowing your child to use this app.

- **Twitter:** Often used for news and other media, this app can also be used to find pornography. A Twitter account is not needed to access Twitter content. I do not recommend allowing your child to use this app. In 2021, Twitter added a type of safety mode that allows users to block abusive content. But, like in all social media apps, users can easily stumble upon dangerous content that may include topics such as suicide, cutting, eating disorders, and violence.

- **Omegle:** Omegle is a chat room that I found out about years ago by accident. My son was lured onto it by an ad, and I found two creepy men with their shirts off trying to chat with him. This app makes it easy for children to be exposed to strangers and nudity, and it is famous for being a playground for sexual predators. I do not recommend allowing your child to use this app.

- **Hoop:** Users are encouraged to make new friends with strangers all over the world. It's almost like a friend dating app. By swiping through profiles, children can choose a person and start a chat. Children can also request each other's Snapchat handles in this app. I do not recommend allowing your child to use this app.

- **Kik:** Kik is a free instant messaging/chat app with a wide array of exposure risks for children. Similar to other messaging apps, this is an attractive app for predators. I do not recommend allowing your child to use this app.

- **Whisper:** This is an anonymous app focused on sharing personal secrets and meeting new people. It is risky and known as one of the favorite sites for predators. I do not recommend allowing your child to use this app.

- **Vault apps:** Vault apps are a category of apps used to hide photos and videos on all of your child's devices without you knowing. Sometimes the icon that appears on your child's phone is a pretend calendar or fake clock. You wouldn't even notice this if you were not looking for it.

  For example, Calculator+ is a vault app that hides files behind a functioning calculator app. Calculator+ can be found in the App Store, and it's free to download. It says, "Safe for everyone," but I disagree. Most of these apps have a passcode, so even if you do check your child's phone and find something like this, you would need the code to access it. Anything your child is trying to hide from you at this level is a bad idea.

THE DANGERS OF ONLINE GAMING

Any gaming platform that allows players to chat with other players is a safety hazard. Gaming platforms such as Xbox, PlayStation, Nintendo, Android Play Store, and PC- or Mac-based platforms offer a way for friends and strangers to directly message children. For example, Roblox is a popular video game; children as young as four years old play it. It has characters and settings for users to explore, play, and build. But Roblox is more than a game. It also serves as a platform that hosts user-created games. There is really no way of checking out hundreds of thousands of user-generated games on your own. Some user-generated content is completely inappropriate for children and can include nudity, sexual acts, and rape scenes. As with most games and apps, there is a way for friends and strangers to directly message children. Predators can also buy in-app gifts and tokens that they can give to other users.

If you allow your child to use these platforms, keep a close eye on who they are chatting with. Also consider changing the parent-control settings. For example, on your Xbox:

1. Sign in to your Xbox account.

2. Select "My account."

3. Select "Security, family, forums."

4. Select "Xbox 360 Online Safety."

5. Select the account you want to control.

6. Select "Allowed" or "Blocked" next to the areas you want to limit or allow access to, and then tap or click "Save."

Each platform is different, but most let you block online chats and messages.

STAY UPDATED

Apps, gaming platforms, and social media platforms change frequently. The following are resources where you can get information on the latest changes and new products.

- **Bark Technology Assessment** (https://bark-o-matic.com/) I love this app and use it in my home. Bark helps parents and guardians monitor texts, apps, social media, and web searches.

  This app is an affordable tool for watching children's online activities for dangerous or unsafe content. Bark is not perfect and is not a substitute for active conversations with children on safety and prevention, but it is a good supplemental tool and can provide a digital safety net for families. Bark also has a safer phone option for families. Their phones for children come with pre-installed Bark technology. Technology changes quickly. To see how serious the problem of online safety is, read this report: https://www.bark.us/annual-report-2021/

- **Common Sense Education** (https://www.commonsense.org/education) This is an excellent place to learn how to keep children safe online with healthy communication and advocacy. It is designed in three segments: parents, schools, and advocates.

- **Common Sense Media** (https://www.commonsensemedia.org/) They combine research with advocacy to make the digital world a safer place for families. Some advocacy work done by this organization focuses on legislation, technology, and keeping tech companies in check and accountable for safe content. They also rate books, podcasts, shows, movies, and help families make smarter choices about the content they consume and help families make healthy entertainment choices.

- **Gabb Phone** (https://gabbwireless.com/product/gabb-phone-z2/) This is a parent-designed "dumb" phone that looks like a smartphone. Gabb phones have parental GPS tracking and can be used for calls and texts, but they do not allow apps to access WiFi or the internet. Children are not able to send or receive photos or participate in group chats. This is a great way for parents and guardians to keep in touch with their children and know where they are at all times.

- **Cybersecurity and Infrastructure Security Agency (CISA) Parent and Educator Resources** (https://www.cisa.gov/publication/cisa-cybersecurity-aware-ness-program-parent-and-educator-resources) This is a website of the US government that provides resources and information on cyber safety for families and educators.

I also recommend that parents and guardians connect with Fareedah Shaheed (2022) and join the Safe Kids Movement. Her website (https://www.cyberfareedah.com) offers information on holistic digital safety for parents and other adults. She makes the topic of online safety realistic and comprehensive. She updates her research and stays on the cutting edge of changes and trends that you need to know about. And you can sign up for text alerts! There is a lot to learn and know, but you don't have to do this alone. According to Shaheed, "The most important thing about cyber safety is active communication with your kids and supervision." Talk to your children constantly. Ask questions and encourage communication and trust. Talk, talk, talk!

Children need to know that, while most people are good in this world, there are criminals lurking out there in cyber land who have specific intentions to hurt children and families. Empower your children with prevention strategies to protect them.

Online Safety Tips for Educators

At school, online safety is just as important as it is at home. Even if your school has parents or guardians sign a waiver to allow the school to post student photos on school websites, do not participate. Frequently, teachers post class pictures or photos of children with identifying information. Taking photos of children in front of your preschool as they wear school shirts and tagging those images with location markers and hashtags is dangerous. You don't want to invite predators to your school. Once you post a child's face on any social media platform, that image can be manipulated, copied, and sold.

Instead, share photos of children with families on private teacher accounts in services such as Shutterfly. Sharing digital photos can be more secure on these sites because members can only see images if they are invited. Make sure your passwords are strong and the company you use to share photos has solid security. Many schools use private, closed-network apps to share photos, newsletters, or emails to families. If you do share an image of a child publicly, blur the child's face or cover it with an emoji.

Classroom Online Safety Rules

Children

- I will stay away from unsafe websites.

- I won't click on any pop-ups.

- If I make a mistake, I will ask for help.

- If I see an inappropriate picture, I will turn off the screen and tell a safe adult.

- If I have any problems, I will ask for help.

Educators

- We will have safety filters on our computers.

- We will monitor the children on the computer.

- We will help if children need help.

- We expect mistakes to happen.

- Children can tell us anything, and we will help with no judgment.

- Children's safety is our first concern.

Many schools offer access to computers or tablets in the classroom. Establish rules and measures to guard children when they use these devices.

- Make sure the device is in a central location that you can easily observe.

- Protect any device the children use with software and firewalls.

- Enable blocks to keep children from accessing unsafe sites.

- Reinforce your pop-up blocker settings. (Pop-ups are a common problem at schools. Kids can easily click a pop-up ad by accident and land on an inappropriate website.)

- Post online classroom safety rules near the computer, and review the rules and procedures often.

- Talk to the children about online risks.

- Reassure them that parents and teachers are always there to help.

Teach children what to do if they find themselves on an unsafe site or if they bump into upsetting images, such as pornography.

- Turn off the screen or look away.

- Alert the teacher of a red flag on the computer or tablet.

- Provide support if the child is scared or traumatized by the picture or video they saw.

- Send a note home to the family and follow up with a phone call.

- Alert your administration about the safety concern on the computer or tablet.

Use the incident as a teachable moment: Kevin had a red flag on the computer, but he followed our class safety rules! Kevin, share with our class what you did to get help.

Review the safety steps, praise Kevin, and check with the children for comprehension.

✗ ✗ ✗

I realize I may have completely scared you with this chapter. I'm scared too! I'm sorry to say that this is a rapidly changing world and our children are at risk. It is a scary world to bring a child up in and there are many challenges. I take the stance that we have to prepare—not scare—our children. The great news is that, with your knowledge of these facts and information, you can get ahead of the risk and prevent harm. We are moving on to how to empower and prepare! I don't know about you, but I feel like I want to take a few action steps right about now.

In the next chapter we will begin to learn about how to teach children about body safety. If you need to go grab your children's cellphones and devices and start inspecting, deleting, and evaluating, go ahead. Take a break, take a breath, and then do an assessment of how safe your family is online. Remember, this is not a time to get mad or upset with yourself or your children. It is a time to evaluate and engage in safer online practices.

Chapter 8

Teaching Children about Body Safety

Hopefully, you have taken that seventh-inning stretch and are ready to move toward prevention and how to actually teach children about body safety. I know that last chapter was tough to read! It was tough to write. And things change so quickly in the online world; you blink, and there is a new app or show to watch out for. I appreciate your dedication to protecting children. Learning these facts, statistics, and the magnitude of child sexual abuse can trigger fear and overwhelm. If you keep reading, you will gain many tools and strategies to overcome these fears. The next few chapters will focus on body-safety rules, identifying feelings, consent, and communication. When speaking to parents online, in my parenting groups, or after a book reading, everyone always brings up the concern of sex ed. And, sometimes all the misunderstandings and political voices in the space take away from the reality that children really do need to learn about their bodies in a developmentally appropriate way. Let's sort through some of these topics.

This Is *Not* Sex Education, and the Three Classic Questions Children Always Ask

There is a lot of controversy these days about what is and is not appropriate to teach to children.

Parents and teachers must learn about gender, gender identity, and gender expression, and it is important to be prepared for these conversations if they come up and to be aware of the school policy, curriculum, and parents' rights. All of these conversations must be handled carefully and in a developmentally appropriate way. Every child needs to be loved, supported, and accepted. We also must remember that children are creative individuals who love playing, dressing up, imitating others, and expressing themselves.

In early childhood education, conversations are not so much about gender and sexual development as they are about teaching empathy. Sexual-abuse prevention focuses on body autonomy, consent, boundaries, anatomically correct words for body parts, safe adults, identifying feelings, and communication skills. Body safety, which is part of many curricula across the United States and is required in many states, is appropriate for children under the age of eight. But, you can learn about body safety at any age. It is never too early or too late to start talking about protecting children. Many parents and guardians start teaching their children about body safety when they are toddlers. All work that focuses on body safety in an age-appropriate way is the very beginning of learning about the human body and keeping it safe.

As I've shared, I am a kindergarten teacher, and I get three sex-related questions from children every single year. Yes, this happens every year, and it always makes me laugh!

- What is sex?

- What is a virgin?

- What does *gay* mean?

What is sex? I usually say, "That is a really great question! Why do you want to know about that?" Once I understand where the child's question is coming from, I might explain, "Sex is what you are born with based on your DNA and chromosomes. Your sex can be male or female. If you have any more specific questions, ask your parent or guardian."

What is a virgin? I definitely don't want to explain this term to a five-year-old, so I get a bit tricky here to avoid it. I say, "A *version* is a different way to tell a story. Any more specific questions, ask your parent or guardian."

What is *gay*? Because this has to do with sexuality and sexual preference, I pass this one off with a different definition for the word. "*Gay* is another way of saying somebody is happy." I am pro-family in all the forms families might take. The reason for the redirect is that I want to avoid confusing the child or saying something that might offend the family. These types of discussions are best held in collaboration with the child's family.

Beyond these answers, I try to figure out the root of the questions. This could be an attempt to disclose abuse. I send the parents or guardians an email or call them at home to chat.

The problem is that some parents and guardians do not teach their children about body safety or sexual education. (I had those parents!) I remember learning in fourth grade that girls get their periods. I was horrified! I ran home to ask my mom why nobody had told me this. She said I didn't need to know yet. Let's face it, not all parents or guardians are comfortable talking about sex and sexual development with their children. Many adults are triggered and scared to talk about the topic because they have their own emotional trauma. If you are feeling behind the curve on any sex ed conversation, don't be embarrassed. It is never too late to learn, and understanding human sexual development is a big part of being an inclusive, helpful, safe adult.

Keep in mind that body-safety skills can create a power shift and keep children safe. We can help prevent child sexual abuse by learning the facts, eliminating the risks, and educating our families. Together, we can take power away from the abuser and empower our families with a prevention toolbox.

It's easy to tackle this often tricky topic if we start early and use the right tools. And it doesn't have to be scary! I don't want anyone to get stuck in fear. We can begin to lay the foundation of prevention education and get ahead to protect our families with a few simple steps.

Let's start today! It doesn't matter how old or young children are. These safety skills are practical for any child who understands language. The earlier you start, the better, and the sooner you reduce the risk.

"Cookies" and "Willies": Doctor Words and Why We Need to Use Them

Many of us have goofy names that we teach our children about their private parts. Go ahead! Take a minute to write down every silly word or slang word you have ever heard for a private part. And try to remember where you heard it or how you learned it.

Guess what? If you are feeling awkward or uncomfortable, you are not alone. Many parents and teachers feel a little strange about using anatomically correct words. This discomfort is something we all have to get over. We must overcome these feelings because knowing and using the correct terms helps protect children in many critical ways.

If you are a brand-new teacher, or even a seasoned one, pay attention here. One, two, three, eyes on me! (That's a little teacher humor.) This story alone can save a child from harm. I learned this critical lesson during my first two weeks of teaching.

I didn't know what to expect during my first teaching job. I was scared stiff on day one. Who were these children, and would they listen to me? Would they learn anything? Enter "Safety Freak" Kim. Would I panic and leave a kid in the bathroom during a fire drill? Would I lose a child on a field trip? Would somebody puke? Would I puke? Yes, that was wholehearted panicking—but I was wholly dedicated to helping these little five-year-old sweethearts. My minimum goals for success were simple:

- **Goal number one:** Cause no harm. Nobody dies or gets seriously injured while in my care.

- **Goal number two:** Don't lose anybody.

If the children learned anything during those first two weeks, that would be a bonus! I was extremely overwhelmed and realized I actually should have read that book on the required graduate-school reading list called *Assertive Discipline* (Canter, 2009). My classroom was chaotic and complex.

I had a teaching assistant to help me. We figured out our schedules and learned the personalities and names of the children. Things were calming down. Things were good. Until they weren't.

During that first week of school, a little girl tugged my shirt and said, "Miss King, my dad took my cookie." I was busy. I looked at the little girl and said, "I'm sorry your dad took your cookie, but you know it's okay to share." I said that! And I went about my business helping somebody pick out a book to read. I did not think anything of this conversation.

The little girl returned the next day and tugged on my shirt again. She said, "Miss King, my dad took my cookie . . . and it hurts." A rush of panic and fear came over me as the dots connected. I realized that this child might be talking about something terrible. I asked her to point to where the cookie was, and she pointed to her private areas. I hugged the little girl and thanked her for telling me. I told her she was very brave and I would help her. I called the school nurse.

As a mandated reporter, a teacher *must* report all suspicions and disclosures of sexual abuse to the school's appropriate chain of command because it is our duty as responsible adults. **You don't have to be sure. You don't have to have evidence.** Many teachers worry about reporting suspicions. What if your suspicions are wrong? When you make a report, child protective services investigates. Validating, analyzing, and verifying a report or suspicion is not your job. But, as a teacher, you are a mandated reporter, so you must report all suspicions and disclosures.

The memory of mishandling my first disclosure has haunted me. This is why knowing the correct terms for the body parts is critical. If this child had said, "Miss King, my dad touched my vagina," or even "Miss King, my dad touched my private parts," I would've known what she meant.

Top Ten Reasons to Learn the Words

1. **Everyone understands the anatomically correct terms.** In each language, the "doctor words" are universal, and there is no confusion with these words. The anatomically correct words and the term "private parts" are things that every adult understands. Every child needs to know these terms. Slang terms can delay reporting and be dangerous. In my case, it prevented me from getting that girl to safety for twenty-four hours. You don't want your child, or any child, to get stuck in a position where she cannot report or disclose quickly and efficiently.

2. **Knowing the terms provides layers of protection against predators.**
    How? Predators are looking for easy targets and easy victims. A child who is well-versed in body safety and body boundaries and knows the anatomically correct terms of private parts is going to be a red flag for that predator. That predator will know just by a few simple conversations that the child won't keep a secret, knows the names of the body parts, and has body boundaries. Therefore, that child is not a good target. That child is too risky. That child knows too much. Sadly, the predator likely will move on to an easier target. A predator is looking for a child who will keep secrets, knows nothing, and won't tell anybody because predators don't want to get caught.

3. **Why wouldn't you?** I can't figure out one good reason not to know all the private parts by the correct terms. The awkwardness over using the terms *vagina* or *penis* stems from associations and baggage that we, the adults, have. Children don't come into this world with body shame, negative word associations, or emotional baggage. They learn them.

    Children don't feel awkward over these words. If you, as an adult, are too uncomfortable to use appropriate terminology at home or school, at least make sure your children know what they are. You can review the anatomically correct words and diagrams in the resource section on pages 112-113.

4. **It's science!** *Vagina, vulva, breast, nipples, scrotum, penis, anus,* and so on are the scientific names of our body parts. Normalizing the anatomically correct words right from the beginning shifts the attitudes and associations over these words. A commonsense attitude toward the body makes things less complicated when children reach the various developmental stages and need to learn about sex, sexual identity, and contraception. Plus, learning about the body is incredibly fascinating. The human body is a beautiful thing. And, after all, these body parts are just as typical and healthy as other body parts; they are just private parts with special rules. They need to be kept protected because they are sensitive.

5. **Knowing the terms takes away the shame from these body parts.** When adults use and teach slang to children, there can be a negative connotation. These words imply that we can't speak of these parts because they're too embarrassing or shameful. Children might think their bodies are embarrassing. Body parts are body parts, and children need to learn to love them.

6. **Children learn to respect their bodies.** When we accept and normalize talking about private body parts, there is no room for them to be associated with shame and stigma. Hence, children start to appreciate and respect their bodies. As young children learn body autonomy, consent, and body-boundary rules, they are empowered to protect their bodies! And, sometimes, they can speak up when others need protecting as well.

7. **Reporting incidents of child sexual abuse is easier and quicker.** One of the most important reasons children must know the anatomically correct names of all of their body parts, especially their private body parts, is because reporting a case of sexual abuse a child might encounter becomes easier. When a child reports to a grownup using words that all grownups understand, the report can be clear and not misinterpreted or missed all together.

8. **Knowing the terms promotes effective communication between parents and children.** Parents openly and honestly discussing genitals and private-parts rules with their children creates a healthy, positive family dynamic. When things get tough on this topic, your child will be more likely to ask for help and feel more comfortable. You want your children to come to you when they need help and to trust that you will help them in a judgment-free zone. You want your child to think, "Oh no! This is so bad! I have to tell Mom!" not, "Mom is gonna kill me!"

9. **Knowing the terms promotes learning about the opposite sex.** This is especially powerful when children are curious. We want to encourage curiosity and normalize the parts of the body. It is okay for a girl to learn all about the boy parts and vice versa. Along with that knowledge comes a reinforcement of body boundaries and rules.

10. **Knowing the terms provides an easy transition to sex education.** Many parents, teachers, and school systems wait to talk about sex ed until children are around the third or fourth grade. However, knowing more detailed information about the body is only going to empower children. As a mom, I explained these topics in a matter-of-fact way and left out intricate details that wouldn't make sense to my five-year-old. As my children grew up, I added more description and detail when I felt it was needed. Introducing the basics, including anatomically correct names of the body parts, helps with later conversations. Eventually, children will learn about gender, sexuality, contraception, function, and more! A solid foundation is essential for a smooth transition to the teen years and will ease communication during the tween and teen years.

If you have a bilingual classroom, or even one student in your class who speaks a language other than English, take it upon yourself to reach out to the parents or guardians and ask them to help you learn the words for body parts in the children's home languages. Explain why you need to know the translations. If you are not comfortable with that, head over to Google Translate. In addition, many child-advocacy centers have resources and can put you in touch with a volunteer or counselor to help you translate or answer any questions. Getting to know your students and families and taking this extra step can help the children and their families feel supported.

Children with disabilities are more than three times more likely to have experienced violence in their lives than nondisabled children. More specifically, children with mental or intellectual impairments seem to have a higher prevalence and risk of violence than do children with other types of disability (Jones et al., 2012). Children with disabilities can be more vulnerable to child sexual abuse for a variety of reasons. Children with communication problems are especially difficult to protect. Collaborate with the family, student services, school social workers, child advocacy centers, and special education departments to develop a nonverbal safety plan. This may include suggesting books to the family, developing a body-safety communication chart, or using technology to assist in reporting.

Sometimes, parents and caregivers make assumptions about children with disorders such as autism or Down syndrome. I had a parent of a child in my class opt out of my body-safety lesson recently. The mom's reasoning what that their child who is autistic didn't need to know about things like the anatomically correct words or consent because these are things her child will never understand. I had to politely disagree. My nephew has autism, and he knows right from wrong. He is more than capable of learning rules. In fact, he likes rules because they help make things clear for him. I use the same rules and strategies in my classroom. Maybe I won't teach my Body-Safety Rules all at once to a child with autism, but I will break the rules down and teach one rule at a time and provide extra hands-on activities for the child to do at school and at home to reinforce the lesson. I encourage parents to use visual aids at home, review safety strategies more, and gather as many books and body safety songs as they can find. Giving up on body safety because a child has a disability helps increase the risk of abuse. We don't want that.

Doctor Words: Anatomically Correct English Terms

There is a lot to know about our amazing bodies! We are covering the basics here, and then some of this stuff children will learn when they are older. For now, these are some of the important "doctor" words you would find in a dictionary or anatomy book. It is important to know the correct words so that any trusted adult can understand in the event a child has a problem.

 Girls _____

Anus: An opening at the end of the digestive tract. It's where the poop comes out. Boys and girls both have this part.

Buttocks: The part of the body a person sits on. Everybody has one!

Chest: A girl's chest develops breasts as she gets older. Breasts are located on the front of the chest and are also known as mammary glands.

Labia: Two pairs of skin flaps that are part of the vulva and located outside the vagina. *Labia* is the Latin word for "lips."

Nipples: Two darker, small, circle-shaped parts of the breast or chest.

Urethra: The part of a girl's body where the pee comes out.

Vagina: The canal that leads from the uterus to the outside of the body.

Vulva: The outside part of a girl's private parts located underneath the underpants. *Vulva* is the Latin word for "covering." The vulva is between the legs and covers the opening to the vagina and other parts inside.

Boys

Anus: An opening at the end of the digestive tract. It's where the poop comes out. Boys and girls both have this part.

Buttocks: The part of the body a person sits on. Everybody has one!

Chest: Like girls, boys have chests and nipples, but most boys don't consider their chests private. Boys usually go swimming with just bathing trunks and bare chests.

Nipples: Two darker, small, circle-shaped parts of the chest.

Penis: The part of a boy's body where pee comes out. It is also an outside male sex organ and part of the reproductive system.

Scrotum: The sac or pouch of skin that contains the testicles; located beneath the penis.

Testicles: The male glands that are contained in the scrotum. They produce male sex hormones.

Bodies are amazing and complicated. We all have parts of our bodies that we don't know much about. It is always okay to ask questions if there is something that you or a child doesn't understand. Would visuals help? You can find a great visual aid in the book *Your Whole Body: From Your Head to Your Toes, and Everything in Between!* by Lizzie DeYoung Charbonneau.

Write down the silly words your children use now or you have heard at school. Talk about these words with your family and introduce the anatomically correct words today.

As you can see, your role as an empowered and safe adult is so important. You can help prevent child sexual abuse by implementing these strategies. You have the power to stop a predator, receive a report, and protect children. My hope is that you now understand why learning the words and helping children learn and use them is critical to safety. Acknowledging your possible uncomfortable feelings here is powerful. If you are uncomfortable, that is okay. But, I encourage you to explore your feelings of unease and talk about them. Many of us have been taught to keep our feelings inside, to bury them, and not to talk about the tough stuff. We don't like feeling uncomfortable, but feeling uncomfortable and expressing our feelings is a must in body safety.

In the next chapter, you will learn the importance of recognizing and labeling feelings. Exploring emotions is one of the most empowering skills children and adults can learn. So, take your stretch or go for that walk. Then, get ready to feel your feelings.

Chapter 9

How Recognizing and Naming Feelings Can Keep Children Safe

Data on how sexual offenders choose their victims are scary but powerful; we can learn so much—and take immediate action. In numerous studies, many offenders claim that they have a way of identifying vulnerable children with low self-esteem and a lack of knowledge about body safety (Conte, Wolf, and Smith, 1989). Abusers identify a vulnerability, fill a void, groom the child, use the child, and desensitize the child from inappropriate touch. They then take advantage of the child further by manipulating feelings such as fear, guilt, and shame, thus keeping the victim quiet. Children can end up believing that the abuse was their own fault. Low self-esteem has been found to be the cause of feelings of guilt and shame among sexually abused children because perpetrators manipulated the children to believe that it was their fault they were abused (Mutavi et al., 2018).

This information from multiple sex offenders screams at me that we must focus on communication and building up children's self-esteem. We must concentrate on helping children develop the ability to identify their feelings and express them confidently, loud and clear.

Communication Is Key

At home, pump up the vocabulary and talk more. Parents and guardians can start immediately by developing vocabulary to label feelings with their children. For example, instead of asking, "How was your day at school, honey?" which often elicits the response, "Fine," try asking open-ended questions such as these:

"Tell me which part of your day made you feel excited."

"Which part of your day made you feel happy?"

"Where do you feel happy in your body?"

"Did you have anything at school that made you feel nervous?" If the answer is yes, continue the conversation:

"Tell me more about that. Where did you feel those nerves?"

"Sometimes I get that too; it feels like butterflies in my tummy. Sometimes adults call that *anxiety*. I used to feel anxiety at school because there was a mean kid in my class."

Use a communication journal with your child as part of your day. In a child-friendly journal, write or draw together. You can use writing prompts such as the following:

- Draw a picture of the best part of your day. Let's think of some feeling words.

- Draw a picture of the worst part of your day. Let's think of some feeling words.

- Draw a picture of a problem you had in your day. How did you solve it?

- Draw a picture of an uncomfortable feeling. What makes you feel uncomfortable?

- What makes you feel strong?

- If anybody makes you feel bad, what do you do?

- If somebody does something that makes you feel good, what do you do?

- Who helped you today? How did that feel?

- Who shared with you today? How did that feel?

- Who got in trouble today? What did they do?

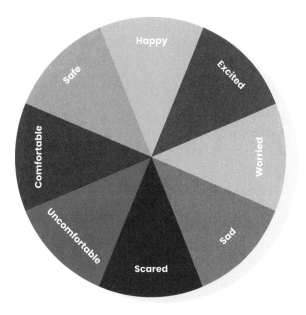

At school, we can make social-emotional learning part of our daily routine. Teachers can be so creative and supportive in fostering emotional wellness and awareness. In a typical kindergarten class, we see examples of social-emotional learning all around. At students' desks, you can find discrete mood charts.

Upon entering the classroom, the first thing many kindergartners do is a feeling check in: "Move your clip to check in with yourself and me." The child typically has three choices, sad, okay, and happy. Many teachers add a Talk to Me clip and a compliment circle to encourage communication and develop positive self-esteem.

TALK TO ME CLIP

To make these, use clothespins, draw lips on them, and clip them to a poster near your desk. The Talk to Me clip is an excellent way for a child to signal to a safe adult that they need a conference to discuss something that is bothering them. The child simply puts the clip on their clothing or hands it to the teacher.

At the beginning of the year, read *Some Parts Are NOT for Sharing* by Julie Federico (2009). Show the children a Talk to Me clip, and explain that the clip is a way to talk to the teacher about urgent things and big problems, such as if somebody hurt them or asked them to keep a secret or if they were sad or needed help at home or school.

Also give examples of what the clip is *not* for, such as, "Lina looked at my paper," "Tommy used my purple crayon," or "Jessica is singing in my ear." Explain that these problems are little problems that the children can solve themselves. Practice brainstorming how to solve these problems. For example, ask, "How can we solve the problem of Jessica singing your ear?" Ask the class for solutions. They might suggest moving away from her, asking her to sing more softly, singing with her, telling her you like her singing but not in your ear, and so on.

Remind the class that the clip is for emergencies, such as the following:

You are about to have diarrhea!

Somebody hurt your body.

Somebody broke a body boundary.

There is a danger.

These are *big* problems that children will need help from safe adults to solve. Make a whole-group activity out of this discussion by sorting a list of problems into one of two categories: Big Problem or Little Problem. Ask each child to give you a problem, and ask the class where to put it. Put problems sorted on a poster or on the board.

COMPLIMENT CIRCLE

The students all sit in a circle. Each student gets a turn to give a compliment to another child, such as, "I like the way Shannon shared with me," or "I like the way Emily helped me with my journal." At the end of the compliment, the circle teacher compliments everyone, then sends home a compliment certificate or award. The children love this activity and start giving compliments to each other randomly.

A classroom rich with social-emotional support can be vital to children who don't have this kind of instruction or environment at home. And for students with well-developed social-emotional skills, these activities serve as reinforcement.

My Top Five Feelings Books

Doerrfeld, Cori. 2018. *The Rabbit Listened*. New York: Dial Books for Young Readers.

This is a wonderful read for everyone. *The Rabbit Listened* is a story that beautifully shares the importance of just listening, and does so in a way that children can appreciate and love.

Emery, Christine A. 2018. *The Black Cloud Blues*. Virginia Beach, VA: Koehler Kids.

The Black Cloud Blues is a gentle way to introduce children to the concept of anxiety and depression and to how asking for help with your problems is a good place to start.

Lee, Britney Winn. 2019. *The Boy with Big, Big Feelings*. Minneapolis, MN: Beaming Books.

What a wonderful job this book does at capturing emotions, and with a male character too! I love that the story focuses on a young boy and his emotions, because boys are often told not to cry or told to get tough.

Willems, Mo. 2004. *Knuffle Bunny: A Cautionary Tale*. Glendale, CA: Hyperion Books for Children.

The funniest story about what happens when Dad takes over for a day. Dealing with panic, frustration, and anxiety leads to a save-the-day moment when Knuffle Bunny is found.

Witek, Jo. 2014. *In My Heart: A Book of Feelings*. New York: Abrams Appleseed.

This book is a must for schools and children's bookshelves. I love the die-cut heart concept that decreases in size as the book proceeds. This book is a beautiful teaching tool. The story explains emotions in a simple and yet authentic way. It can be read by individual readers, but it may be more effective for a whole-group reading activity to start a conversation about emotions.

FEELING WORD WALL

A word wall typically has all of the students' names, color words, number words, and some of the Dolch high-frequency words that the teacher introduces on a set schedule. To this, I add feeling words too.

Patricia Cunningham (2016), the inventor of the world wall, says, "You just don't have a word wall; you DO a word wall." It is an active, lively, memorable, and fun activity. I love the word wall for feeling words because we use all sorts of activities to help the children engage and have fun with each word and its meaning, which helps children remember the word and use it confidently.

Most teachers have word walls in the classroom to help develop early reading skills. You can choose a feeling word to add to the word wall each week, or send home a list of feeling words. Ask your students to go on a word hunt at home for feelings. They can circle words they find, or if they can write, ask them to write the words on index cards or paper. You can add each of these new feeling words to the word wall.

For example, a child brings in the word *anxious*. Write the word on a sentence strip. Then, ask the class to help here with some letter cheering. Lettering cheering is something I did as a kindergarten student at Wolfpit School way back in 1975! I do not know who invented this fun, but I thank her! This activity is always a big hit with the children in my classroom.

YOU: Give me an *A*.

CHILDREN: *A*!

Give me an *N*. *N*!

Give me an *X*. *X*!

Give me an *I*. *I*!

Give me an *O*. *O*!

Give me a *U*. *U*!

Give me an *S*. *S*!

YOU: What does it spell?

CHILDREN: Anxious!

Say it louder. Anxious!!

Say it in a whisper . . .

Say it like a cowboy. . .

Say it like you are scared. . .

Say it like you are happy. . .

Say it like you are confused. . .

Weave in as many ways to say it as you can stand. Then, cut the word on the sentence strip into individual letters and scramble them on the floor. Ask a helper to put the letters back in order to spell the word. Write that word on a sentence strip again and put it on the word wall.

Ask the students if they know what that word means. *Anxious* means "worried" or "uneasy."

Invite the children to write or draw about the word in their journals: I feel anxious when. . .

✗ ✗ ✗

When we build a strong foundation of recognizing and labeling our feelings and then sharing them, we create emotionally secure children. When children learn and practice these skills at home and school, it fosters the development of positive self-esteem. With practice, children can become excellent communicators who know when to speak up for themselves.

We know predators are looking for easy targets. Let's make it difficult for them!

Chapter 10

Body-Bubble Boundaries and Body-Safety Rules

"Building a culture of communication based on feelings, connection, and support is how we protect our kids!"

— Kimberly King

Consent has become a buzzword that stirs controversy these days. Many adults assume that we are referring to sex and the ability to give consent to sexual activities. But at the core of consent is a practice many children learn at home and preschool. So take a breath; you are probably already teaching consent without knowing it. Consent education starts with the idea that we should respect one another's rules, boundaries, and space. We are not talking about sex or sexual activity at all, because children cannot consent to sexual activity. Following rules and respecting boundaries helps us stay safe and get along with each other. Teaching children about consent can actually help keep them safe from sexual abuse. Many parents and educators of young children aren't comfortable using the word *consent*, and that is okay. If you are uncomfortable with using that word, the best idea is to use a simple, clear, and consistent vocabulary that everyone understands. You can use the word *permission* and then add *consent* when ready.

Teaching children the concepts of body autonomy and consent are critical skills, as they are the foundation of body-safety education. When I introduce the topic of consent to my class, I usually begin with a brainstorming session to assess what the children already know about the subject. Consent is often associated with sex, but it simply means giving permission. When teaching this concept to young children, it focuses on a variety of nonsexual scenarios, such as hugs, kisses, borrowing items, and sharing. I repeat: Sex and sexual education are not part of the conversation on body-safety education for young children. However, teaching consent concepts does have the purpose or ultimate goal of prevention. We begin a lifelong conversation on consent with children by introducing body boundaries and body autonomy.

The Body Bubble

I start by teaching children to imagine that they have a giant bubble around their bodies. Within that body bubble is their personal space, and nobody is allowed to touch them without their permission. Consent means the child gives permission for someone to give them a hug, kiss, or physical touch. If using the word *permission* feels more natural, go with that.

Everyday examples of consent can be found at home and school. Let's take tickling, for instance. If a child is being tickled and says, "Please stop!" that means they do not consent; they do not give permission for the tickling to continue. It should raise a red flag if somebody tries to look at, touch, tickle, kiss, or play games with private parts. If a red flag is raised, it means that the child feels unsafe and is having an unsafe touch or body-bubble violation, and they would come and tell a parent or a safe adult as soon as possible. Another example can be found in roughhousing or wrestling. If your son is wrestling with his cousins, and he starts to become uncomfortable with the physical touch or roughness of the play, he can say "Stop," or "I don't want to play anymore." At that point, all the children playing with your son should stop. If they don't, your son would need to create an exit strategy and get help from a safe adult. (We explore creating exit strategies in chapter 11.)

The one thing I stress with families is that children cannot consent to anything concerning private parts. Because of this, doctor visits become a significant example of how parents and children must work together on body safety. When your child goes to the doctor, remember that sexual abuse can only happen with time, opportunity, and unsupervised access. Many parents blindly trust doctors because they are in a position of authority. But, abusers are often attracted to these roles of trust and access.

A doctor should never be alone in an exam room with a child of any age. This is a huge red flag!

An informed, empowered parent or guardian with the child in an exam room is the only way to have a safe appointment and protect the child. Children can learn at an early age that only specific trusted adults can help them care for their bodies. The doctor visit is excellent place to model body-safety rules. Parents can explain to their children that the doctor may examine their private parts to ensure they are healthy, but only if a mommy or daddy (or guardian) is in the room and the child says it is okay. Even doctors need consent! The parent and the child need to give permission to a doctor who examines the body's private areas. Why? Say it with me: Because children cannot consent to anything involving private parts.

Teaching Children to Say No

As we talk about body boundaries, it is essential to teach children to identify their feelings and use assertive language to say no. I like to review all the different ways the children can say no. I also explain to them that even a maybe is not a yes. Take a peek at the list at right and follow the lesson plans on pages 137-140 to teach children how to say no and listen to the no. There is an incredible opportunity to build a strong foundation of consent at a young age.

Ways to Say Yes and No

No!	Yes!
No way!	Okay.
I don't think so.	Certainly.
I don't want to.	Absolutely.
Nope.	I'm sure.
Not now.	You bet.
Not today.	Thumbs up with a yes
Not really.	I said yes.
Thumbs down	I will.
I'm not sure.	I want to.
Maybe.	Happy to.
I'm not in the mood.	I would love to.
I said no!	
No answer	

Understanding consent will follow children through the tween years and into adulthood. You can model consent in your home and your classroom with ease.

Intentionally teach children that, when somebody doesn't listen to their *no*, they can raise a red flag. We find our voice when we figure out how to identify our feelings and speak up when somebody violates a body boundary rule. These early childhood empowerment techniques can become a part of the child's identity and help their voice become more assertive and decisive.

When children learn to connect with emotional intelligence, they genuinely understand their self-worth. They begin to understand at an early age that they are the boss of their body, that they have rights, and that they can even speak up and say no to adults.

When should we start teaching our children about consent? You can start modeling consent as soon as your child understands language. There are many natural ways to teach and model consent at home. For example, during potty training and diaper changes, modeling consent is about the narrative and the way cleaning or coaching is conducted. The parent models a quick, easy, no-nonsense diaper change technique. There is no funny business.

> MOM: Honey, I will quickly change your diaper to get you cleaned up, okay? One, two, quick wipe! Zip, zap . . . all done.

There is no reason to do anything else but clean up and get moving.

Other ways to model consent during diaper changes and potty training include the following:

> "Would you like Mommy [Daddy, Grandma, or other trusted adult] to help you with the potty?"

> "Would you like to do that all by yourself?"

> "Oops, it looks like you missed a spot. Do you want to try again, or can Mommy [Daddy, Grandma, or other trusted adult] help?"

> "Here is one more wipe; you are almost squeaky clean."

Obviously, diaper changes and potty training are mandatory health and hygiene practices. But these practices also offer opportunities to introduce and model consent conversations in a light and supportive way.

SAFETY NOTE

I don't recommend leaving four-year-olds in a tub alone because this would be unsafe. But you can pull the shower curtain halfway across and sit quietly in the bathroom or stand by the door to ensure your child is supervised and safe in the water.

Bath time is also a perfect opportunity to introduce or review consent. Your four-year-old might want a little privacy when taking a bath. You can ask your child if they would like you to stay in the bathroom with them and talk. Or you can ask them if they need any help. You then allow them to say yes or no. You could ask, "Do you feel comfortable with me standing in the bathroom? Or would you feel more comfortable with me sitting just outside the door?" Also, bath time is a great opportunity to introduce the anatomically correct words for all of their parts.

As you practice these conversations, you start to help your children learn communication skills and gain independence. They will learn how to speak up for themselves regarding privacy and practice consent.

The Importance of *No* Means No

Parents and guardians, do you have trouble saying no to your kids? If you tell your child, "No snacks before dinner," do you stick to the no? Or does your child negotiate and lawyer their way to that brownie? When you tell your child, "No more screens for the night," do you hear, "Come on, Mom, please? Last night, you let me use it till eight o'clock. That's not fair."

We have all said no and then changed our minds. If the kids really pester, bug, and persist enough, sometimes we just say yes because we want them to stop bothering us. Sometimes, it is easier to give in. But, these are powerful opportunities to teach them that *no* means no.

Point out that you said no, and point out the negotiation attempts. Remind them that *no* means stop asking and stop pressuring. Enforcing the no at your home will help your child enforce their own no. The ability to say no and hear a no is critical to your child's safety.

Teachable moments begin at a young age with private-part safety. Families can teach their children how to clean their bodies and care for themselves, which will help them develop independence and self-esteem and provide perfect opportunities to model consent. Keep the conversation simple, and take every opportunity to give your child choices and verbal feedback full of praise. Emphasizing a predictable routine focuses on keeping the entire body clean and safe while using accurate vocabulary and thinking skills. For example, consider the following bathroom conversations.

MOM (modeling consent): I'm going to help you wipe because it looks like you missed a spot. Is that okay?

CHILD: Okay.

MOM (encouraging thinking and recalling body safety training): Why is that okay?

CHILD: Because you asked me, and you are helping me stay clean.

MOM (reinforcing vocabulary): What part is this?

CHILD: That's my anus. It's where I poop.

Bath time can be fun. You can make up silly songs to review body safety and boundaries simultaneously.

MOM: It's bath time. I am here to help you because I have to keep an eye on you when you are in the water. Once you are old enough, you can take a bath all by yourself. Do you have your washcloth and bubbles?

Here is the washcloth. Cleaning time! Can find your fingers? Can you wash them?

Can you find your elbows? Can you clean them?

Where are your knees? Can you clean them too?

(Remind your little one to clean their private parts toward the end of the bath.)

MOM (later): Do you need help finding your towel?

CHILD: No. I can do it myself. I can dry myself.

MOM: Okay great! I'll drain the tub. Call me if you need me.

CHILD: I'm a big kid! I am going to put my PJs on too!

MOM: Wow! That's great! You're doing an excellent job of taking care of your body and your things.

You can review the "doctor words" with your child in the context of the entire body. The simplest way to address the matter is to teach that if the body part is under a bathing suit or underwear, it is private and has special functions and rules. The mouth is also a private part.

You can teach your children to identify their feelings and use red and green flags as symbols. At home, you can reinforce this strategy daily. We are keeping the lines of communication about feelings open. A fun an easy way to review is to sing one of the body-safety songs from Body Safety Songs (https://bodysafetysongs.org/?page_id=5) and review body-part terms after the song you sing.

Establishing Body-Safety Rules

I like to keep things simple with body-safety rules. At school, after teaching children and talking about body safety, I post the rules and share them with families. Body-safety rules can be posted on the fridge at home, in the classroom, in the bathroom, on notes for babysitters, in the child's notebook, and in a newsletter to families. I also suggest that parents and guardians give body-safety books and the body-safety rules to everyone who spends time with their child. When people know you are in a body-safe classroom or home, this adds a layer of protection. Predators are looking to groom families who know nothing and find children who are easy to trick and manipulate. When you empower the home and school family with body-safety rules, you create a force field!

11 Body-Safety Rules

1. I use the correct names for my body parts.

2. I am the boss of my body.

3. I can say no to hugs, kisses, or unwanted touch.

4. Nobody can look at, touch, tickle, or play games with my private parts.

5. I can't look at, touch, tickle, or play games with other people's private parts—including family members and friends.

6. I keep my private parts private.

7. I never keep secrets—especially about private parts!

8. I will tell a safe adult immediately if someone tries to see, touch, tickle, or play games with my private parts or asks me to see, touch, tickle, or play games with theirs.

9. I trust my instincts! If something doesn't feel right, it's probably not right.

10. If I have a body-safety problem, it's never too late to tell!

11. If somebody violates my body boundary, it is not my fault—ever! So, go tell!

Sometimes, children can feel unsafe, worried, or scared about many topics they encounter during the day. Helping them learn feeling words will ease understanding. Trust and open communication can quickly happen when a child can identify feelings and communicate effectively.

SAHAR: Mom, today, I told my teacher there was a red flag on the playground.

MOM (remaining calm and asking an open-ended question): What happened? Can you tell me more?

SAHAR: Tommy pulled down his pants and showed people his private parts. I put up a red flag!

MOM: That was brave. Tell me more.

SAHAR: Because what he did broke our safety rules. I was worried and uncomfortable, so I followed our safety plan.

MOM: What did you do next?

SAHAR: I left and went to tell my trusted adult, my teacher.

MOM (using praise, validation): Wow! You did such an excellent job following our safety plan. You helped yourself and Tommy stay safe. I am so proud of you. Did you feel okay telling?

SAHAR: I did! And Tommy even told me not to tell, and he said it wasn't a big deal!

MOM: Good for you! You knew what to do. It is a big deal. So proud of you! Do you want to talk some more about it today?

SAHAR: Nope. I'm good.

MOM: Okay. Well, I am so glad you identified the red flag and followed our safety plan. I love to hear about all the parts of your day! Thanks for telling me.

BOOKS TO SPARK DISCUSSION

Researcher Eleanor Craig (2022) reviewed forty-four children's books written to help prevent child sexual abuse. (Note: This study is ongoing and will be updated as new books come to market.) Craig focused on specific criteria deemed effective in preventing child sexual abuse, such as maintaining boundaries and personal space, teaching correct anatomical names for body parts, distinguishing between appropriate and inappropriate touching, and teaching children what to do if they feel uncomfortable. Of the books reviewed, Craig found seven that met the criteria:

Fleming, Latasha. 2015. *Know Tiny Secrets: How to Keep Your Body Private and Safe*. Scotts Valley, CA: Create Space.

Girard, Linda W. 1984. *My Body Is Private*. Park Ridge, IL: Albert Whitman and Co.

Holcomb, Justin, and Lindsey Holcomb. 2015. *God Made All of Me: A Book to Help Children Protect Their Bodies*. Greensboro, NC: New Growth Press.

Jessie. 1991. *Please Tell! A Child's Story about Sexual Abuse*. Center City, MN: Hazelden.

King, Zack, and Kimberly King. 2020. *I Said NO! A Kid-to-Kid Guide to Keeping Private Parts Private*. Weaverville, CA: Boulden Publishing.

Sanders, Jayneen. 2011. *Some Secrets Should Never Be Kept*. Victoria, Australia: UpLoad Publishing.

Sanders, Jayneen. 2016. *My Body! What I Say Goes!* Victoria, Australia: Educate to Empower Publishing.

In choosing a book for children, Craig recommends selecting both storybooks and information books. Before sharing a book with a child, an adult should always read it to make sure that the content is appropriate and to prepare for questions the child may have afterward. Ideally, the selection of books should include those designed to be read with an adult as well as those intended for children to read on their own. Once you have familiarized yourself with the facts, you can sit down with your child and talk about this topic in a calm way. Take a look at the following sample conversation.

ADULT: Hey, kids, let's sit down and chat about something really important. You know how I always make you two wear your seat belts in the car and your helmets when you ride bikes?

CHILD: Yes! I don't like my helmet. It makes me hot.

ADULT: I know. I don't really like them either, but they protect our brains. Without a helmet you could get really hurt.

CHILDREN: We *know*!

ADULT: Well, there is another thing that has to do with keeping your body safe. It's more than protecting your brain. It's protecting your whole body. It's called body safety.

CHILD: Are you gonna make us wear a whole-body helmet?

ADULT: No! But I could wrap you up in bubble wrap. Just kidding.

CHILD: Okay, what is body safety?

ADULT: It's just us learning about our bodies and talking about how to keep them safe. I've been reading books and learning about it, and I want you to learn about it too.

CHILD: Do you mean safe from bullies?

ADULT: Well, body safety can keep you safe from bullies. I'm really talking about tricky people who try to touch kids' private parts.

CHILDREN: Ewww! Gross.

ADULT: Sometimes adults or other kids try to touch kids. It is unsafe. So, we are going to start talking about ways to keep safe and protect our bodies. We are going to learn lots of things and keep talking about it.

CHILD: I have a friend who takes karate to stay safe. Can we take karate?

ADULT: Maybe. Karate is a great sport and really helps kids get fit and learn ways to protect themselves. We can talk about that later.

CHILD: Okay.

ADULT: Let's start by learning more about our bodies. Here is a great book called *Your Whole Body Book* by Lizzie DeYoung Charbonneau. We're going to read this book tonight before bed and see what we can learn. I bet there are things in this book that I don't even know.

CHILD: Really?

ADULT: Really. Back when I was a kid, we didn't talk about our bodies very much. I think Grandma was embarrassed about this stuff. But, we all have bodies, and we all need to know how they work and what our parts are called.

CHILDREN: Why? That sounds gross!

ADULT: Because knowing the names of your parts and how they work helps you understand how incredible you and your body are. And, it can also keep you safe from creepy or tricky people. Kids who know a lot about body safety are kind of like kids who wear seat belts and bike helmets. They have a layer of safety to protect them.

CHILD: But my friend had a bike helmet and still skinned her knee!

ADULT: Yes, a bike helmet won't protect your knee. But, a skinned knee heals up quick. You can still have accidents and get hurt even if you wear a helmet or buckle up. Taking safety steps helps you avoid really big hurts.

CHILD: You mean I may skin my knee if I fall, but my brain won't be broken?

ADULT: Yes, exactly! So with body safety, the same thing applies. You might have a situation where you feel unsafe, but you will be more protected than other kids because you have learned body-safety skills.

CHILDREN: And karate? Please! Karate?

ADULT: Okay, I will look into karate! Now let's read! And remember to stop me along the way if you have any questions or need to tell me anything.

I recommend reading a children's book first by yourself. Then, come up with a script to introduce the rule or concept. Chat about the rule before you read the book. Find out what your children already know. Read the book slowly and encourage questions and conversation. At the end of the book, check for comprehension. Talk more about the contents of the book. What did you like? What did you dislike? What did you learn?

Teaching Consent at School

In the classroom, you can model consent in several ways with any question you ask. If you are getting ready to go outside on the playground in the winter, you can ask a student, "Would you like some help zipping up your coat?" This sounds simple, but it is the beginning of consent communication. You can draw attention to this by asking, "Would you like me to help you with your coat, or would you like to do that yourself?" And then you can ask, "What is that called when somebody asks you if you would like help?" Engage the child or children in a conversation to remind them of the body bubble and permission or consent.

Outside, you may spot children giving consent on the playground when a child asks permission to play chasing games, push someone on the swings, or play in the sandbox

My Top Five Body-Safety Books

I also have a few favorite body books to help you tackle this topic easily and learn some things yourself!

Diggs, Krystaelynne S. 2021. *Where Hands Go: An Introduction to Safe and Unsafe Touch*. Independently published.
(Ages 3–8) An excellent resource for parents, teachers, therapists, and guardians who want to talk about body safety with younger children. This book is beautifully illustrated and easy to read with young children. The author does a great job explaining the importance of body boundaries and autonomy in a clear and child-friendly way.

Federico, Julie K. 2009. *Some Parts Are NOT for Sharing*. London, UK: Tate Publishing.
(Ages 6 months+) An adorable, simple story with a pair of friendly fish as the main characters. Children learn about boundaries and appropriate touch in a nonthreatening way. Parents and caregivers will love the simple, straightforward language. This book is also available in Spanish.

King, Zack, and Kimberly King. 2020. *I Said NO! A Kid-to-Kid Guide to Keeping Private Parts Private*. Weaverville, CA: Boulden Publishing.

Morrison, Eleanor. 2018. *C Is for Consent*. Phonics with Finn.
(Ages 2–4) This book teaches that it is okay for children to say no to hugs and kisses and will help them become comfortable with expressing physical boundaries.

Shoatz, Shariea. 2019. *My Voice Is My Superpower*. Independently Published.
(Ages 3–10) A story of body safety and friends helping each other when they realize they need to help a friend report abuse. Children teaching each other and sharing prevention strategies in a calm and supportive way.

Starishevsky, Jill. 2020. *My Body Belongs to Me/Mi cuerpo me pertenece*. Minneapolis, MN: Free Spirit Publishing.
(Ages 3–8) In English and Spanish, this book helps children learn how to tell someone if they do not want to be touched, or if an unwanted touch has already happened, how to tell a trusted adult with confidence. Body boundaries, unwanted touch, and how to tell a trusted adult are covered with clarity.

with a friend. When you recognize these actions, praise the children for asking permission and receiving a yes or no.

Toileting is another opportunity to teach consent. Teaching children how to wipe and clean themselves and how to wash hands helps them develop independence.

But potty problems happen at school. Teachers must deal with bathroom accidents and learn how to handle these events with consent and safety procedures in mind. Emphasize a predictable routine that focuses on getting clean and safe with no shame. We don't want to shame a five-year-old for having an accident, especially when they are starting to feel like a "big kid." Simple conversations are comfortable here. For a teacher, it might sound like this:

STUDENT: Miss King, I had an accident! Help me!

I always use the rule of two in these situations. As a reminder, the rule of two means that one child will never be alone with one adult. Abuse can only happen with isolation, time, and opportunity. When there are two adults present at all times, the risk is eliminated. And, as a teacher, you do need to protect yourself. This safety practice protects you in the unlikely event a child says you did something that raised a red flag. Everyone is safe and wins if you have a second adult with you as you deal with potty issues.

TEACHER: Yes, Susan, I'll help you. You stay put, and I will get Miss Julie [the teaching assistant] to work with us to help you. How about you put everything in this bag, and then I will pass you your clean clothes. (Hand a plastic bag to the child.)

Depending on the level of the bathroom situation, that may be enough. But if there is a problematic situation and the child requires serious cleaning, you have some choices to make and things to consider.

- Call the child's parent or guardian, and keep the child safe and observable in the bathroom. The parent or guardian may prefer to handle this herself.

- Ask the adult and the child what they would like you to do.

- You can pass wipes, and the child can clean up.

- You can assist, if needed, with another staff member observing you. (Make sure to wear gloves.) The parent and child need to consent if you help the child clean up after a potty accident.

WHOLE-GROUP ACTIVITY: MISS JULIE LOVES HUGS!

This is a fun activity that you can act out in front of the class. Using the script below as a guide, and adding to it as needed, can be really silly and engaging for the children. This role-playing situation had my class in hysterics!

WHAT TO DO

Ahead of time, ask two children to participate in the following scene. Tell them what to do. You will also need some bubble solution for an outdoor follow-up to this scene.

Gather the children for a whole-group activity. Tell them that you and your assistant teacher (or another adult volunteer) will act out the following scene.

Setting: The morning meeting has just started in your classroom, and Miss Julie, the teaching assistant, comes barging into the class and heads right over to the teacher and gives her a giant, tight, excited hug! (Make this even more fun by having "Miss Julie" use a loud voice and a distinct accent.)

> MISS JULIE: Hi, Miss King! Sorry I'm late! I was parking my car. I need my morning hug! I just love hugs. I love hugging everyone!
>
> MISS KING (Stiffly standing there looking at the class): Hi, Miss Julie! Um . . . I don't like hugs. I like high fives.
>
> MISS JULIE (Continuing to hug Miss King, who looks at the class with an uncomfortable expression): You like hugs! Everyone likes hugs. (She hugs tighter and Miss King makes a worried face.)
>
> MISS KING: I don't like that! You are in my body bubble! That makes me feel uncomfortable!
>
> MISS JULIE (In a soft voice): Uncomfortable? Bubbles? You are being silly! Kids, Miss King likes hugs, doesn't she?
>
> CHILDREN: (Some say yes. Some say no. Some are giggling.)
>
> MISS KING (Shakes her head no): Miss Julie! I don't like that! (Modeling a loud, assertive voice): I don't want a hug. Stop! No hugs. Respect the bubble.

MISS JULIE (Stops hugging): Wait. Oh . . . okay. I'm sorry. I just love you sooooo much. (Julie pauses for a moment and then goes in for another hug.) Hey! But you hugged me yesterday! So you said okay yesterday, so . . . (More hugs)

MISS KING: Today, I do *not* want a hug. When you want to hug somebody, Miss Julie, you have to ask! Because only some people wish to hug. Only some people like hugs all the time.

MISS JULIE: I can't believe it! Let's ask the kids! Should I hug Miss King? Why? (Call on a few volunteers; preselect children to answer, if needed.) Oh, good answer! I'm getting it now. How many of you like hugs all the time?

CHILDREN: (A few raise their hands; preselect children to participate in the following exchange)

CHILD 1: I do! I love hugs all the time.

MISS JULIE: Yay! Then, I can hug you now? (Rushes over to hug)

CHILD 1: If you ask me!

MISS JULIE: Here comes a big hug! I'm so happy. Miss King doesn't like hugs.

CHILD 1: Miss Julie! Miss Julie! You forgot again.

MISS JULIE: What? Forgot what?

CHILD 1: You have to ask me for a hug, and I have to say yes!

MISS JULIE: What? All these rules are confusing.

MISS KING: In our class, we always ask permission to hug our friends. If a friend says yes, that means they give us consent. If a friend says no, we do not have permission to hug. We always want to listen to our friends and respect their body bubble. Not everyone likes hugs and being close to people all the time.

MISS JULIE (to CHILD 1): Okay. Fine. [Name], can I please have a little hug?

CHILD 1: Yes! (Miss Julie gets a quick hug.)

MISS KING: Can anybody tell Miss Julie what a body bubble is?

CHILD 2: It's an imaginary bubble around your body. You are the boss of your body bubble. If anybody wants to hug you, they have to ask permission.

MISS JULIE: Let's get some bubbles and imagine our own big, personal body bubbles around us. Let's go outside first and blow some giant bubbles.

Extension Activities:

- Invite the children to write or draw a journal entry about body bubbles.

- Have a body-safety circle chat at the end of the day. Review the hugs lesson and how to say yes or no.

START A CONSENT CHAIN

Create a consent chain with the children, and use it to decorate your classroom. Math and writing opportunities abound, and this a social-emotional learning gem!

Materials:

- Construction paper

- Scissors

- Tape or stapler

- Marker

- Cut the construction paper to make 500 strips.

- Keep the strips, tape or stapler, and a marker handy. Every time you catch somebody giving or asking for consent, ask them to write their names on a strip. Loop the strip to make a link and secure it with tape or a staple.

- Start a chain by adding links. Hang up the chain all around your room. This chain will eventually go down the hallway!

- At the end of the year, you can make a big day of acknowledging how well the children did with asking for consent!

Extension Activities:

- Writing workshop: Invite the children to make a big class book on consent and body bubbles. Invite each child to write their own unique book on consent.

- Math:

  ▸ Estimate how many links are in the consent chain. Chart the predictions on a piece of chart paper.

  ▸ Divide children into groups and have them start counting and keeping a tally of their count.

  ▸ Encourage them to group by fives and tens and to practice counting by fives and tens. Add all of the counts together to get a total tally of links. Report the results.

Teaching Body Safety at School

It's easy to teach children about their bodies and safety from the beginning. As you empower them with the body-safety rules, you will teach them about their bodies too. The topic just organically presents itself.

WITH VERY YOUNG CHILDREN

For all care providers, changing a diaper properly and safely is critical. Make sure you reach out to parents and share your existing safety procedures and policies. Parents and guardians, if you have already started narrating consent language with your baby or toddler, share that practice with the care provider. A simple, consent-focused diaper change might sound like this:

> "Okay, honey, you have a wet diaper, so we are going to do a quick diaper change so we keep your private parts safe and clean. Here is the wipe mom sent. Mom said she changes you when you have a wet diaper. I'm opening your diaper. Wipe, wipe, wipe! Mom says always wipe front to back."

> As you toss the old diaper and grab the new one, you can say something like, "When you are a little older, you will be able to do all of cleaning for yourself. But for now, your parents and I have to help keep you safe and clean."

Talking a child through a diaper change can help them feel more comfortable. But, let's face it, this is not consent. Babies don't get to consent or not consent to diaper changes. When caregivers at home and at school communicate about procedures and safety, the building blocks for consent are put down. Narrating a diaper change can provide comfort and predictability to a child and can help them learn what a safe diaper change or help with the potty should look like.

WITH OLDER CHILDREN

Starting at the beginning of the year, we can integrate social-emotional learning with daily check-ins. When we put feelings, boundaries, body autonomy, and body-safety rules together, children learn how to communicate when they have a red flag or a body-safety problem.

For a teacher, the opportunities to talk with children will look different from those at home.

Depending on the development of each child, the home environment, and the parenting style, rules may be harder to comprehend for some children. And often, school may be the first place where some children encounter concrete rules. Parents and guardians have a great opportunity to be part of the process and help their child understand, learn, and contribute to a safe classroom based on rules.

Yes, there will be challenges. Rules can be abstract and hard to understand for young children. For instance, what does "Don't yell" mean to a three-year-old? Instead, try simple but clear rules such as, "Use an inside voice." Then, model what an inside voice sounds like, and model what an outside voice sounds like. Show children the difference. Experiment with volume levels so everyone understands what you mean.

Rules need to be specific and clear and taught and modeled in a consistent way over time. After you set your basic classroom rules, move on to body-safety rules. Brainstorming rules with the children gives them ownership of the rules and consequences. Take a few minutes to brainstorm with your class five of the body-safety rules. Help them get the important body-safety rules you would like to see in the class. It is a great idea to do this within the first week of school.

Teaching about Red Flags

When you are trying to teach children to "Raise a red flag," some can take this literally. So make sure to start with the concrete rules you can demonstrate. For example, if you are teaching that private parts are those located under a bathing suit, bring a visual aid. Try using a doll in a bathing suit or a picture of children wearing bathing suits. Have a conversation about all the different types of bathing suits. Talk about the differences between most boys' and girls' bathing suits. Explain that the areas covered by bathing suits have special rules. (The mouth does too; we'll get to that in a few minutes.)

Next, introduce the visual of a red flag. Explain that a red flag is "raised in your head" whenever a child feels unsafe or uncomfortable. Tell them that if somebody makes them feel unsafe or uncomfortable, they can always tell you, "I had a red flag," and you will make sure to take time listen to their problem and help them if needed. Teaching rules in a classroom takes practice, dedication, effort, and consistency. Learning rules takes time, support, and positive reinforcement. Consider the following examples.

ACCIDENTAL CONTACT

SHANNON: Miss King, Missy, touched my private parts. I had a red flag!

MISS KING (providing immediate support and straightforward communication): What? Oh dear! Well, thank you for telling me you had a red flag. Let's talk about it. Can you tell me what happened?

SHANNON: Yes! Okay, I was jumping rope with her, and her hand bumped into my bathing suit area. My private parts!

MISS KING: Hmm. Do you think that her hand accidentally brushed up against your parts while you were jumping? Or did she do it on purpose?

SHANNON: I don't know. Maybe it was an accident.

MISS KING: Let's ask her what happened. Is that okay with you?

SHANNON: Okay.

MISS KING: Missy, Shannon said you touched her private parts. Can you tell us what happened?

MISSY: I was twirling the rope for her, and she jumped really close to me, and my hand touched her by accident. I said I was sorry.

MISS KING: Okay. Shannon, do you think this sounds like an accident? You were playing jump rope, and your bodies got too close. Her hand reached too close to you. Does that sound about right?

SHANNON: Yes. I think it was an accident, and she said sorry right away.

MISS KING: Okay, I am so glad you told me because whenever there is a red flag in our class, we have to check it out to ensure everyone feels safe. Thank you for telling me you felt worried. That was exactly the right thing to do. Do you feel safe and comfortable?

SHANNON: Yes. I am going back to jumping rope. I will stay in the middle this time and give myself more space.

MISS KING: Excellent idea!

In this case, the teacher provided support, asked open-ended questions, and reinforced the importance of helping to keep everyone safe by talking to a trusted adult when something upsetting or scary happens.

BATHROOM SCENARIO

On the one hand, learning about the body and how it works is fascinating to children. They can spend hours exploring everything from the inside of their nose to the toenails on their toes. Curiosity is completely normal, and exploring private parts and asking questions is developmentally appropriate. However, children must also respect others' body bubbles and accept a *no* when it is given.

SHANE: Do you want to see my ding-a-ling?

JAMES: Um, no! That's a red flag! We don't show private parts to friends.

SHANE: But it's fun, and it can do tricks!

JAMES: No! I said no!

SHANE: Too late!

Shane pulls down his pants and chases James around in the bathroom.

JAMES: Red flag! Stop! I am out of here!

He runs out to the hallway to tell his teacher.

MISS KING: What's wrong, James?

JAMES: Shane pulled down his pants and chased me with his penis, and he didn't listen to me or the rules.

MISS KING: That sounds scary and very upsetting. What should we do?

JAMES: I don't know, but he is gross! I want to go home.

MISS KING: We can let your mom know what happened. I am sorry he grossed you out and scared you, but you did the right thing. You yelled *stop*, and you left the bathroom.

JAMES: He does this all the time to other kids too! He thinks he is funny.

MISS KING: Okay, I will read the class a body safety book today, and we will review the rules. If he can't follow our safety rules, he won't be able to go to the bathroom when other people are in there. I guess I will have to send Miss Julie to stand guard at the door. I hope you will stay at school today. You can sit at my desk today if that makes you feel safer. What do you need to feel less worried and more comfortable?

JAMES: Can Miss Julie stand guard at the door the next time I go to the boys' room?

MISS KING: Sure! If that makes you feel safe today, you bet!

In this instance, the teacher immediately addresses the child's cry for help. She gives him an opportunity to offer a rule-based kid-generated solution, and she reassures him that he took the right steps by yelling *stop* and leaving the bathroom. Next, she tells him the steps she will take to address the problem, and she offers ways for him to feel safe at school.

KISSING

Some sexual-abuse prevention educators include talking about the mouth as a private part. I am one of those educators. Why? Because without including the mouth as a private area, an abuser can trick a child into abuse involving the mouth. Kissing on the lips and kissing of body parts can be part of grooming process that desensitizes a child to intimate touch. I know it is disgusting to think about. But, we have to think about how predators think to get ahead of them. Also worth noting is that the mouth can be a place where signs of sexual abuse, such as rashes around the mouth and sores on the lips and in the mouth, can be seen. So, kissing is something we have to address.

I have seen plenty of parents kiss their children on the mouth during my time as a kindergarten teacher. And I do understand that there are cultural differences to consider. I am not making any judgments on this. Every family is different. It is important to include the discussion of kissing because it can be used in grooming and, just like hugs, requires consent.

TANYA: Miss King, Donell asked me to kiss his butt! Red flag!

MISS KING: Thanks for telling me, Tanya. That is definitely a red flag. How did you know to tell me?

TANYA: Because kissing people is private. And we don't kiss people at school. And my mom told me the only thing that goes in our mouth is food, and the only thing that comes out should be kindness and breath. And butts are private! And kissing somebody's butt is gross. And breaks rules.

MISS KING: Oh, wow! I like what your mom told you. Kissing, tongues, and mouths are just as private as bathing-suit parts. You might give your mom, dad, and grandma a kiss goodnight, or you might give them a hug and a kiss. But you get to decide who you kiss and who you hug.

You are the boss of your body. And we don't kiss people at school. And we don't lick things or people at school.

TANYA: Boys are gross. They always talk about butts and awful stuff.

MISS KING: Sometimes boys and girls talk about icky, yucky, red-flag things. So, my job is to teach everybody the body-safety rules. I am going to speak with Donell. Would you like to come with me and tell him you don't like what he said to you and that it was a red flag?

TANYA: Yes. I am going to tell him.

MISS KING: Okay, I will come with you.

TANYA: Donell, I don't like how you talked to me today. You made me feel uncomfortable and broke our body-safety rules.

DONELL: I was just joking.

TANYA: It's not funny, and it's a red flag.

MISS KING: Donell, we need to review body-safety rules together after lunch. We want everyone to feel safe and comfortable in our class.

In this scenario, the teacher supports Tanya in problem-solving and brainstorming what to do, which in turn supports self-advocacy. She reviews the safety rules with Donell and redirects his behavior. One way to do this is to separate the two children temporarily to provide space. She brings Donell with her to the reading center and gets him started on an audiobook with a different friend. She asks Tanya what she would like to do now. She suggests spending some time in the block center, starting a painting, or helping set up for snack.

COMPUTER RED FLAGS

Make sure your computers and tablets are in observable space. With young children, this is critical. All schools with computers and online access for children should have programs and filters to ensure safety. But, nothing is foolproof, and children can encounter online pornography and violent content with a click. Teach the children that, before turning on any device, they should check with their teacher or parent first. Online safety is so important for children. Post a few simple rules by the computer.

Rules for Online Safety

- I will only turn on this device with an adult watching me.

- I won't click on pop-ups.

- If I accidentally click on something that is unsafe, such as a naked picture or video, I will look away and go tell my safe adult.

- Mistakes happen! Always ask for help if you need it.

- Stay on the app or site that your teacher or adult has turned on with you.

- Don't surf the internet! Surfing is not safe for children.

- Don't talk, text, or message anybody while you are online.

It is also a good idea to show children how to turn off the screen quickly in the event of a red flag. A great book to help with this topic is *Good Pictures, Bad Pictures Jr.: A Simple Plan to Protect Young Minds* by Kristen A. Jenson.

> KEVIN: Miss King, I clicked on this thing here, and there are red flags! Help!
>
> MISS KING: Thank you for telling me. What did you do to get rid of the red-flag pictures?
>
> KEVIN: I looked away and turned the screen off! That is our school safety plan for computers.
>
> MISS KING: I'm sorry the computer gave you a red flag. It is not your fault. Next time, if something pops up, ask me first.
>
> KEVIN: It looked like part of the phonics game!
>
> MISS KING: Tricky people! Red-flag people are sneaky! It was a red-flag computer trick. Not your fault. I have clicked on the wrong button plenty of times. Let's text Mom and tell her what happened.
>
> KEVIN: Good idea. Because I was scared about it.
>
> MISS KING: Do you want to talk about what you saw?
>
> KEVIN: No, I want to talk to my mom and dad.
>
> MISS KING: Okay, let's call.

In this example, the teacher takes immediate action after a red-flag scare, providing proximity, praise, and comfort. She gives the children an opportunity to express his feelings. She also provides him with an opportunity to review the rules and procedure. She offers the opportunity to talk with her immediately or to talk with his parents.

Treats vs. Bribes: What's the Difference?

Classroom behavior plans are usually based on rules, rewards, and consequences. It can be a little tricky for children to learn these systems, and it is important to clarify with your class the difference between rewards or treats and bribes or threats.

Predators use gift giving, bribes, and tricks during the grooming process. Among teachers, parents and guardians, and children, a common understanding of what is safe and what is unsafe is essential. I explain this tough topic to children and families like this: "Sometimes, a teacher might offer children a treat for doing a great job listening, or a neighbor might give a child a cookie just to be friendly. But a bribe is different. A *bribe* is when somebody offers someone money or prizes to do something that they *don't* want to do or wouldn't normally do. And if it has to do with private parts or is unsafe, it is a red flag."

Knowing the difference can help children understand when they need to tell a safe adult about a possible red flag. My book *I Said NO!* offers a child-friendly way to explain bribes without getting too confusing. Also, consider the following:

MISS KING: Good morning, class! Can everyone meet me on the carpet for circle time?

I love the way you all sat down. I'm going to give you all a sticker!

CHILDREN: Yay! Stickers!

MISS KING: What's it called when a teacher gives you a sticker for doing something you normally do that helps our class work better?

CHILDREN: Sticker time? Presents! Our teacher being nice!

MISS KING: Right! That's called a *treat*. How do treats like this make you feel?

CHILDREN: Happy! Good!

MISS KING: Do you feel worried?

CHILDREN: No!

MISS KING: A treat could be something, such as a sticker, that your teacher offers you for doing a great job listening. Or it might be a cookie that your neighbor offers you just to be friendly. That's okay! But a bribe is different. A *bribe* is when somebody offers you money or prizes to do something that you *don't* want to do or wouldn't normally do. A bribe is a red flag. Don't take the bribe. Walk away and tell your parents or another safe adult.

Okay. Let's try another example. Susie, I forgot to clean up all the tables before snack. Cleaning the tables is my job, but I forgot. I'll give you five dollars if you clean up the tables. Is that a treat or a bribe?

SUSIE: I don't take money from grownups. Except for my grandma. She gives me money on my birthday.

MISS KING: Why don't you take money from most other grownups?

SUSIE: Because mom said when grownups give kids money to do something, it is a job. And kids can't work. Our job is school.

MISS KING: But you are at school! So is it okay to take money?

SUSIE: No! That's not okay. Grownups should not give money—except for grandparents on birthdays and stuff.

MISS KING: Did I offer you a bribe?

SUSIE: I think so.

MISS KING: Why?

SUSIE: Because you are offering me money to do something I wouldn't normally do and it is not my job and I don't want to do it.

MISS KING: Yes! Is this a red flag? Should you tell your mom about this when you get home?

SUSIE: Yes!

MISS KING: Okay. I want you to raise your hand when you think there is trouble and somebody is being unsafe or breaking a body-safety rule. Here is another example. Ready? Keyshawn and Jared are in the boys' bathroom. Jared crawls under the divider and into Keyshawn's stall.

CHILDREN: (hands go up)

MISS KING: Jared says, "Keyshawn, I see your privates! Want to see mine?"

CHILDREN: (hands go up further) Red flag!

MISS KING: What should Keyshawn do?

CHILDREN: Say no! Tell Jared to get out! Scream for help. Get out and tell teachers.

MISS KING: Yes! But, then Jared offers Keyshawn a hundred dollars to touch his private parts!

CHILDREN: (all raising and shaking their hands)

MISS KING: What is that called?

CHILDREN: A bribe!

MISS KING: Yes! What should Keyshawn do?

CHILDREN: Yell and tell!

MISS KING: Who should he tell?

CHILDREN: A safe adult! A teacher!

MISS KING: Yes! Can somebody show me how they would tell? Let's act it out. (Rosita raises her hand.) Yes, Rosita. Show us what you would do.

ROSITA: (Walks to classroom door, then walks quickly to teacher) Miss King, I had a red flag!

MISS KING: A red flag! What happened?

ROSITA: My friend broke the safety rules and tried to bribe me.

MISS KING: Which friend? (Rosita points to Susie.)

SUSIE: (laughs) I would never do that!

MISS KING: We know. We are just practicing a tell. Now, can everyone raise their hand if they want to practice a tell? It's important to practice telling. Make sure the adults hear you. And it's important to tell me or any safe adult if you ever had a red flag because we are here to keep you safe! You will never get in trouble for telling about a red flag. Ever!

You may be thinking, "Wait a sec, Kimberly. I bribe my own kids to do chores." Let's just face this one head-on! Most of us bribe our children in one way or another. For example, "If you eat your vegetables, then you can have dessert." "If you go to sleep on time tonight, we will go to the park tomorrow!" "If you get your morning work done, I will give you a sticker!" "If you clean up your toys, I'll let you stay up an extra ten minutes before bed." Or how about, "Let's play the quiet game. The winner gets a prize from the prize box!" We can call those types of if/then statements *behavior modification* or *motivation*. But we are giving them something to get them to do something positive.

For me, the distinction is focused on the purpose. When a parent or teacher gives a child something they would typically offer them as part of an individual behavior plan or class behavior plan, I would call that a reward. Teachers and parents give rewards all the time.

Verbal praise for doing a good job on homework or cleaning their room makes children feel good. Sometimes, offering a special item or treat is needed to motivate a noisy class to settle down or a child to cooperate with the bedtime routine. Creative ideas can help the classroom and the home run smoothly. If we have to add a little incentive to help children make good choices or develop healthy habits, so be it.

When an adult tries to coerce or sway a child into doing something they don't want to do, would not normally do, or is not good for them, it can be referred to as a bribe. Children can be tricked and bribed with prizes, treats, money, time, and special activities. When a bribe involves breaking the private-parts body boundaries, we call that a red-flag bribe. And we teach children to find a safe adult when that happens. Say no, and go!

Unfortunately, predators are master manipulators and can entice, trick, and manipulate young children with relative ease. How do we combat that? We empower children with the truth. If anybody violates their body boundaries and breaks body-safety rules, it is never their fault, and they need to tell us immediately. We will always believe them. We will not be mad. We will love and support them no matter what. We will work to make sure that it doesn't happen again and they will be safe. We are proud that they told us. When children know that they will not be in trouble, judged, or not believed, they are more likely to tell.

I know that explaining the difference between bribes and treats sounds a little over the top. But, talking about these differences plants a seed. It helps children start to question adults when they try to get them to do things. It is okay to question adults and notice these behaviors.

Take a minute to think about how you use rewards, treats, and behavior management. Can you think of a time in your home or in your classroom when you have offered a treat or bribe? Write some of those events down and come up with alternatives for motivating behavior.

Make sure to review with your own children and your class that there is a big difference between a bribe and a treat. If the children are able to write, you can turn this into a writing prompt after you cover the topic in your class.

- Prompt 1: Did you ever have a time when anybody gave you a treat for doing something that you wanted to do and were supposed to do? Let's talk/write about that.

- Prompt 2: Who remembers what a bribe is? Let's talk/write about that today.

- Prompt 3: Has anybody ever offered you a bribe for doing something you *did not* want to do? Let's talk/write about that.

- Prompt 4: Has anybody ever tried to give you a red-flag bribe or made you feel unsafe or uncomfortable? Anybody who wants to talk about that or share their journal can sit in the author chair and share.

✗ ✗ ✗

When a bribe or treat doesn't work, abusers can threaten children. An abuser might say, for example, "If you don't do [bad thing], I will not be your friend," or, "I will tell your parents the touching was your idea." This topic is one we have to discuss with children to keep them safe. And, while preventing child sexual abuse is not a child's responsibility, we do have to prepare children with exit strategies to help them get out of unsafe situations. In the next chapter we will discuss how to teach children about safe exit strategies and develop problem-solving skills using scenarios.

Chapter 11

"What If" Scenarios and Child-Generated Exit Strategies

"What if" scenarios are a great way to help children create ideas and discuss sexual-abuse prevention strategies. Think of the situations that a child might encounter in a typical day. If you are a parent or guardian, jot down the locations and things your child does daily with and without you. If you are an educator, write down a list of risky environments where the children you teach could encounter a threatening situation, such as waiting for a bus, walking home, playground time, or getting separated from the group on a field trip.

Strategies for Everyday Situations

When talking with children about "what if" scenarios, some can be about basic body safety or daily problems children encounter. Discuss the scenario and make a strategy to solve this problem. Consider the following example.

DAD: What if I was late to pick you up at school? What would you think, say, or do?

AJAY: I'm not sure. You're never late.

DAD: What would you think?

AJAY: I would think, "Why is Dad late? What should I do?"

DAD: Let's write down your thoughts.

Together, they brainstorm a list of ideas.

DAD: These are great ideas, Ajay. Now, what would you say to yourself as you wait? What would you say in your head to yourself?

AJAY: I would say to myself, "Dad probably is running late. I will sit still here. If he doesn't come in five minutes, I will go inside and get help from a safe adult."

DAD: Oh, I love this idea! Now, what would you do if I'm still not there after five minutes?

AJAY: I would go to the office and tell them to call you.

DAD: Perfect plan!

When children start thinking through ideas and developing strategies to solve problems, it helps them gain ownership of these ideas. They are then better able to retain, remember, and implement the solutions confidently. Children learn from creative, independent thinking, but they also from repetition. Rehearsing this type of scenario in a child-generated practice is a great way to help the skills, strategies, and solutions sink in.

Let's consider another scenario at school.

MISS KING: Let's practice a body-safety exit strategy to solve a problem on the playground. What would you do if a boy from the first grade was running around the playground with his pants down, and he started chasing you and laughing?

CHILDREN: Ewwww! Gross!

MISS KING: Who wants to help me figure out how we could solve this problem?

ABBY: Me! I know what to do.

MISS KING: Do you want to share your idea with the class?

ABBY: Sure! First, I would tell this kid to stop. And if he didn't, I would trip him and then go tell my teacher.

MISS KING: I like the idea. Why did you decide to trip him?

ABBY: Because I don't want his private parts getting near me and he probably runs fast.

MISS KING: Okay, I understand. Does anybody else have any other ideas?

SANTIAGO: I do!

MISS KING: Okay, Santiago, tell us your exit plan.

SANTIAGO: I would say to this kid, stop! And then he would stop.

MISS KING: I like that you are using your words and being direct. How would you say stop?

SANTIAGO: (yells) Stop!

MISS KING: That is great. Do you know what else you could do there?

SANTIAGO: What?

MISS KING: You could say stop, and then say his name. So, if this kid's name was Kevin, you would yell, "Stop, Kevin!" When you yell a name, it usually gets a teacher's attention. What would you do if he didn't stop?

SANTIAGO: I would run in the direction of a safe adult to get help.

MISS KING: What if a safe adult was all the way across the playground and you were worried? What else could you do?

SANTIAGO: I could get a friend and climb up to the top of the jungle gym.

MISS KING: I love that idea too! Why would you climb the jungle gym?

SANTIAGO: Because it would be hard to climb a jungle gym with your pants down.

MISS KING: Good point, Santiago. I like your thinking here. And why did you bring a friend to the top of the jungle gym?

SANTIAGO: Because we talked about having safety buddies, and two voices could yell for help louder than one voice!

MISS KING: Oh, wow! These are great ideas. But, what about the tripping? Let's talk about that. If it is an emergency, and you feel unsafe, is it okay to push somebody away or trip them to slow them down, if nothing else works and you tried all of your other exit strategies? Let's take a vote to see what our class thinks.

Strategies to Prevent Sexual Abuse

For sexual-abuse prevention scenarios, using the people in your circles as examples is essential because of what we know about perpetrators. About 90 percent of sexual abuse happens with the people we know and trust. And of these abusers, about 60 percent are acquaintances, teachers, neighbors, or community leaders. Thirty percent of children are abused by immediate- or extended-family members (Finkelhor and Shattuck, 2012). Consider the following examples parents or guardians can use.

BABYSITTER SCENARIO

Mom and Dad are out to dinner and a movie. We have a babysitter watching you and your brother. The babysitter wants you to take a bath with your little brother. What should you think, say, and do in this situation? What are some things we should talk about here?

Think: Generate some questions, such as:

- What is our rule here?
- Do we ever take baths in front of babysitters?
- Do you take baths with your brother?
- Do you think Mom and Dad would feel okay about this request?
- Would you feel safe?
- Does this request follow our family safety plan?

Say: Generate some options, such as:

- I want to call Mom and Dad about this.
- Mom and Dad don't like us to take baths together.
- No, I already took a bath.
- I don't take baths when my parents aren't home. It's part of our safety plan.
- No, I am not comfortable with that idea.

Do: Generate some ideas for actions, such as:

- Call Mom and Dad and ask.
- Text Mom or Dad.
- Refuse to take a bath.
- Say, "No thanks. That violates our rules."

PLAYDATE SCENARIO

What if you are at your friend's house, and his older brother wants you guys to come into his room and watch videos? You do, and then you see naked people in the video! What could you think about?

Think: Red flag! Naked videos are not for children.

What could you say?

Say: Naked videos are not safe for kids! I am not watching.

What should you do?

Do: Look away, walk away, go tell a safe adult.

Make sure you tell the safe adult what you saw and talk to your parents about what you saw when you get home.

SLEEPOVER SCENARIO

What should you do if you are at a sleepover and your friend wants to play doctor and look at your private parts?

What could you think?

Think: Red flag! Private parts are private.

What could you say?

Say: I don't play games with my private parts!

What should you do?

Do: Tell your friend you want to play a different game or play outside. If your friend listens to you and follows your body-safety rules and boundaries, you can keep playing. But, if that friend does not listen to you, you need to go tell a safe adult. Be specific with what you tell the safe adult. You can say, "Susan was trying to touch my private parts! I want to go home!" Or, ask to use the phone and call your safe adult and give them your code word: "Spaghetti!"

TICKLING SCENARIO

What if you are playing outside with your uncle, and he is tickling you too much? Let's say that you decide that you want him to stop because you feel uncomfortable.

What should you think?

Think: Red flag! This doesn't feel right. I am going to ask him to stop.

What should you say?

Say: I don't like that. Stop!

What should you do?

Do: If he stops and listens to you, then you have a green flag to keep on playing. But, if he won't stop and doesn't listen to you, then you raise a red flag. Walk away. Go tell your mom or dad or other safe adult.

Expert Advice on Making an Emergency Exit

Jeffrey Konich, a fourth-degree black belt and author of *The Parents Guide to the Black Belt Way* (2022), provides some critical advice in regard to body-safety techniques to teach children. These techniques are helpful to adults as well. In a recent interview, Konich and I spoke about that 10 percent and how to prepare children for an "emergency exit" without scaring them. He explained:

> As a parent, your biggest fear is probably that your child will be harmed in some way. While you can't always be there to protect them, there are some things you can teach them to help them stay safe. Here are the top three things to teach your kids to help prevent them from being snatched by a predator:

> 1. Yell, "Stop!" as you step back into a defensive stance and raise your open hands up in front of your face. This will startle the predator and give you time to get away.

2. Yell things like, "Help! This is not my mom!" or "This is not my dad!" If it's a family member, yell, "No, [family member's name]!" This will alert people nearby that something is wrong and help them find you.

3. Teach your children that they *never* let anyone put their hands on them. Make them repeat this every time you are going anywhere there is a crowd or potential for them to be out of sight even for a moment. This will help them remember what to do if someone tries to grab them. Tell them that, if and only if the person does not listen, they can scratch, elbow, kick, smack, and scream to get help. By teaching your children these simple techniques, you can help keep them safe from predators.

Another great tactic that I learned during one of Konich's body-safety courses is what to do to shift the power of a grab. He suggests that if somebody does try to grab your child (or you), you get low. I mean get your butt on the floor. Apparently, this makes it much harder for the person to move you or make you go anywhere. I actually asked my son, Alex, to try this with me at home to see if it worked. It did! Getting low made my 6-foot, 4-inch, 195-pound basketball player struggle with pulling me anywhere. You can explain this in a child-friendly way by calling this a "sit down strike." Once a person grabs, sit down fast. Then, strike with a kick or block. Konich teaches children to use their legs to kick and block the grabber.

Konich and I also talked about safe places where children could run if they were evading a grab.

He teaches that children should turn and run the other direction. It takes time for the grabber to get in his car and turn his car around on a road, especially when there's traffic. He advises that children run toward a store or gas station, a school, a fast-food restaurant, a police station, a known neighborhood safe place, or even grab the hand of a person who looks safe and is walking by, such as a mom with children. Teach children to make a spectacle of themselves. Be loud!

And teach them to ask to call 911. If there is nowhere to run, he suggests climbing a tree or hiding.

Role play and practice this type of situation at home with the children in the event the 10-percent situation rears its ugly head. A person has a better chance of survival of this type of assault or attempted assault if they don't get in the car. That said, if they do get in the car and find themselves trapped, tell them to not stop thinking of ways to escape. For example, at a tollbooth or stop sign, unlock the door or roll down the window, and get out and run in the opposite direction.

Teach children the sign for help (see image below).

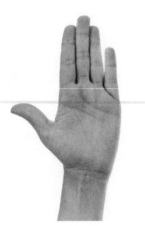

In the event that the abductor and child stop at a restroom or restaurant, practice alerting the staff, faking an illness or medical emergency, spilling a drink, writing a note on a napkin, throwing up (or pretending to throw up), pulling a fire alarm, or going into the kitchen.

Jeffrey also advises that parents teach children to notice things if this situation happens. Look for landmarks, where the sun is, what time it is, license plates, car makes and models, street names, and physical characteristics of the abductor.

When a child is kidnapped, an all-points bulletin (APB) will be issued to all police. Also, an amber alert is issued on the media so everyone is looking for that missing child. Remind children that kidnappers often lie and threaten children. Threats toward other family members can paralyze anybody in a traumatic event like this. A statement from a kidnapper such as, "If you try to escape, I will go to your house and kidnap your brother," is usually a lie. Remind the children that if they get help, the criminal will be caught and arrested.

Talking through these unlikely events may just provide a child or family member with a little clarity to make an escape. For extra security, parents, teach your child how to share their location on their cellphone or tablet. Also consider ways to track your child on a cellphone, tablet, tracking jewelry, or trackers such as AirTags on backpacks.

✗ ✗ ✗

Practicing "what if" scenarios is essential in helping children work through tough circumstances and thinking through problems with ease. But, as we know, children learn through repetition and rehearsal. Teaching them rules without applying those rules to their lives and circumstances makes it harder for them to remember the strategies and skills needed to properly and safely get out of a situation if needed. Obviously, as adults who care for and love children and want to protect them, we try to make safety-conscious decisions that reduce the risk for our children and students. But, practice is key!

Make your "what if" rehearsals personal. Use all of the activities, places, and people they know, and practice. You can even make some silly rehearsals on lighter topics. Support children's critical thinking and problem-solving abilities. "What if" questions can also be helpful in learning how to report abuse, because practicing reinforces the idea that abuse could happen and it is never their fault. Most children rarely report sexual abuse to anybody. The next chapter will help you better understand some of the statistics on telling and why most children never do.

Chapter 12

Children Tell, but We Need to Know the Signs

Physical signs of sexual abuse are not always evident with children. Knowing the signs to look for is extremely important in detecting and assessing child sexual abuse. Receiving a direct tell is possible if children have been adequately educated and empowered in body-safety skills and strategies. However, often children don't come up to us and spill the beans directly: "Dad, my coach has been touching my private parts!" It's usually less direct and may include something more like this: "Dad, I don't want to go to soccer today. I feel sick."

A child victim may keep their abuse secret for many reasons. Aleesha Barlow, founder of @TellSomebodymovement, shared this with me: "Sexual abuse is terrifying, and it is often very confusing to children when dealing with a master manipulator, and abusers lie. They typically use fear, embarrassment, and guilt to keep victims quiet. Sometimes, the abuser will convince the child or young adult that nobody will believe him or that they somehow asked for the abuse and will be punished if anyone finds out about it.

The child may feel somewhat protective about the abuser and not want to betray some misguided 'trust' between them or cause a family to break up over the situation."

The signs of sexual abuse are not always obvious. You must know what to look for as a parent, teacher, or caretaker. Later in this chapter, we will take a closer look at signs that sexual abuse may be happening. Parents who suspect sexual abuse should ask their child directly in a calm and gentle way. And if abuse is suspected, a parent can have the child examined physically by a sexual-abuse specialist.

Open communication is key. Children must be clear about the fact that there are no situations in which a child is *ever* responsible for any sexual interaction with an adult. If you feel something is off or want to check in on this topic, it's always okay to just ask. "Is anything happening with your coach that makes you feel uncomfortable?" "Has anybody ever broken a body-safety rule?" Let's talk about it.

Having sexual-abuse prevention books in your home is also a great conversation starter. Put your books on the coffee table. Read them with your children, and recommend your favorite parenting books and body-safety books to all of your friends, the children's coaches, and their teachers before playdates, sports, and the start of school each year.

While it is not a child's job to protect themselves against a skilled abuser and be responsible for their own safety, knowing simple sexual-abuse prevention strategies can be incredibly empowering and help children and caregivers raise a red flag with a safe adult when a warning sign appears. Understand, too, that when a child and entire family has been groomed and terrorized by an abuser, telling is often too frightening because the abuser threatens to do things such as kill family members and pets.

I reached out to my dear friend and "twin mom" toward the end of writing this book with an idea to see if she would want to share her story publicly. Shariea Shoatz is a mom, an educator, an author, a survivor, and founder of BuddySpeaks.org. She is a victim of child sexual abuse from a family member when she was a young girl. We call each other "twin moms" because we have so many things in common in regard to our children, their problems, our ages, our stories, our struggles, and our passion to protect children.

What we don't have in common is the experience of being groomed by a caregiver, a nanny. Shariea's story is hard to read, but it is worth reading because it puts grooming of a family and grooming and sexual abuse of children into context. Her story will help you understand why children often don't tell.

Trigger Warning

If you are a victim of sexual abuse and have a difficult grooming story, please pause. This may be extremely triggering and difficult to read.

My son was a victim of physical and sexual abuse from our nanny. He started stuttering—extreme stuttering—which I know now was a response to trauma. My son didn't stop stuttering until the year the nanny moved back to the Philippines and we moved back to America. But, I didn't figure out what happened until much later. It took him about six years to tell me.

Looking back, some other more subtle signs were present. My son was always constipated and held bowel movements in. He refused to close the bathroom door or the shower curtain. He always wanted to sleep with the lights on, wanted to sleep in his sister's room, and had frequent nightmares. He started sleeping with stuffed animals as his protectors. He started taking pictures of private parts. Sometimes he overate, and sometimes he didn't eat. One thing I noticed, looking back at pictures, is that during that time he rarely smiled. He was in so much pain both physically and emotionally that he could not smile.

Our nanny was also a caretaker. She showed up and groomed us all from the start. She groomed me first. She studied me and knew what I needed. She was very protective of my son. She took special interest in him. She said things like, "I will make sure he is okay. He stutters. He can't do things on his own, so I will make him safe." She would make his favorite foods. She quickly gained our trust by doing everything to gain it. She groomed our community and was an active and trusted friend and member of the community. She treated all children's friends well. She was very kind on the surface. I was a single mom at the time, and she filled a void. She filled all my needs. She went shopping. I could send her with my credit card, and she never misused it. Never touched our money. She made my life so much easier so that I would trust her like a second parent. She was religious. She cooked, cleaned, shopped, and took care of us all. Sometimes, she called me *Mama*, and at times I thought of her more like a daughter,

On one occasion, I asked her if something was going on with my son because he was touching his penis frequently. My son was crying and whining in his room and playing with his penis constantly. I asked her, "Why is my son touching himself? Did you do something?"

"No, Mama, I would never hurt him!" I believed her. Things slowed down with my son's odd behaviors. She may have backed off at that point with the abuse.

To keep my son quiet, she told him she was going to kill our pets if he even thought about telling on her. I believe she did kill our rabbit and our cat. I can't prove it, but I know. She told my son that assassins were going to come get him and kidnap him. She talked about kidnappers from the Philippines. She tried to make us all believe that kidnapping was real in her country, because she talked about this in front of the adults in the house. It made my son believe it was real. My ex-husband started to suspect that she was a liar and became suspicious.

She made threats to set my son on fire. She also threatened to put poison in the orange juice and kill us all. To this day my son doesn't drink orange juice. She continued to physically, emotionally, and sexually abuse my son. We had no idea. My son loved her and hated her at the same time. We moved back to America and left the nanny before we learned what had happened. The threats were very real and concrete in his mind, even though she didn't work for us anymore or live in the same country.

He started a new school. I picked him up one day, and he said, "Mommy, can you hurry up and take me to Pizza Hut to use the bathroom?" My heart dropped. He was nine at the time, and I thought something must have happened to him at school in the bathroom. We went inside the restaurant.

When he came out of the bathroom, I asked him, "Did something happen in the bathroom [at school] that is making you scared to go?"

"Can I tell you in private?" he asked.

I agreed and drove home. This was the longest thirty minutes of my life.

He said, "Mommy, I am ready to tell you now." He wouldn't look at me.

I told him, "Whatever it is, you will never get in trouble. I will always believe you. I am here. You are safe. This is Mom."

He said, "Mommy, I was scared because I didn't want somebody to touch me in the bathroom like the nanny did."

I told my son that I loved him and that I was so proud that he told me. I thanked him for telling me. He told me more details. He shared that she had told him that if he told me, I was going to kill him, and that it was his fault. She told him that God would never forgive him. She had manipulated him to believe it was his idea and his fault. She made him believe she was pregnant. During the abuse, his brain just shut down and he was living in survival mode.

Seeing an adult in the [school] bathroom had triggered memories and made him scared.

My son is the reason why I created Buddy Speaks. (My son's nickname is Buddy.) For six years, he couldn't tell because he was threatened and terrified. I don't know if he would have ever told if I hadn't ask the questions directly and in a calm and supportive way.

Children trained in body safety know that a body-boundary violation is never their fault.

So why do some children tell and others don't? When a family creates an open, safe, supportive environment to talk about feelings, problems, concerns, worries, sex education, and prevention, children know they can talk about anything. They feel comfortable telling about big problems such as body-boundary violations, as well as the minor issues such as, "My sister stuck her tongue out and looked at me with a weird face."

When children understand body-safety strategies and feel supported, communication flows.

When they know the body-safety rules and know it is never their fault, they feel safe to share a red flag with a trusted adult. Once Shariea's son felt safe and supported, and far enough away from that nanny, he told.

I can't tell you how many parents have emailed me and said, "My son told me he had a red flag yesterday! And while his report made me sad and scared, I can protect him and stop it." Or, "My daughter came home from a playdate and told me her friend's brother showed her a red flag movie online, and I told the mom." Telling can be one of the hardest things for children and adults, unless we make it easier for children to tell us. Often telling seems impossible, dangerous, and scary for children. Many adults carry the secret of sexual abuse to their graves.

Reporting is complicated for most children, and telling takes an incredible amount of self-advocacy and bravery. Researchers estimate that 38 percent of child victims disclose the fact that they have been sexually abused (London et al., 2005; Ullman, 2007). Twenty-six percent of child sexual abuse survivors disclose their abuse to adults, and only 12 percent disclose to the authorities (Lahtinen, Laitila, Korkman, and Ellonen, 2018). Of the 38 percent who do disclose, 40 percent tell a close friend rather than a safe adult or authority figure (Broman-Fulks et al., 2007). There are several reasons why victims of child sexual abuse do not disclose immediately, if at all. These include guilt, fear of family disruption, self-blame, and fear of not being believed (Lemaigre, Taylor, and Gittoes, 2017). When children share about their abuse with a friend, those disclosures don't always end up with a report. This is why it is so critical to train children to report any problems to the safe adults in their lives. The problem of child sexual abuse is bigger than we realize. These statistics are based on reported cases and studies, but the real numbers are impossible to calculate.

When abuse happens within a family, there are several complex reasons why children don't always tell. I spoke with Jane Epstein, founder of Complicated Courage, to learn more about this problem. According to Jane, "Survivors underreport because of feelings of embarrassment and shame connected with the abuse. They may be confused or look up to the older sibling or family member. However, it may be an inability to make rational decisions because of limited cognitive skills, life experiences, and lack of body-safety education." She added one of the categories that nobody talks about: sibling sexual abuse. She encourages all parents and guardians to learn about sibling sexual abuse so they can empower and protect their children.

Reasons Why Children Don't Always Tell

- They may know nothing else, think that sexual abuse is the norm, or do not have the language to express themselves.

- They may be terrified to cause additional family duress.

- They may be protecting a sibling from abuse.

- They may have gone into a freeze state and are not able to access any of these traumatic memories.

- Memories may have been suppressed and can hide in the mind for years or even decades.

- They may be dealing with threats and manipulation from the abuser.

- They may fear that they will not be believed.

- They may figure that nobody cares because nobody ever noticed or asked.

- They may love the abuser, who might be a parent, sibling, or friend, and have complicated and confusing feelings about telling.

During an interview with me on March 23, 2023, survivor and sexual-abuse prevention advocate Irina Mihaela, the founder of the Child Innocence Project, shared her survivor story and why she didn't tell.

> Abuse happens in stages. The first one is grooming. My grandfather groomed me since I was four, gave me my first earrings, and bought me gifts. I must have been fourteen when my grandfather decided it was time for me to learn about sex. He even bought me an anatomy book. He said I needed to be vigilant so boys would not deceive me and leave me pregnant. Six years later, he was still "teaching" me . . . I didn't understand until much later that it was abuse. He was the one I considered safe. My parents fought constantly. My father drank a lot and beat us all. My mom was depressed and critical. What choice did I have? Who to tell? Did my body belong to me? Between physical punishment and sexual abuse, it certainly did not.

In a March 20, 2023, conversation, Angie Berrett, survivor and trauma-informed intuitive movement therapist, shared that if a child is sexually abused by a person in a religious organization, such as a church, "The child may believe telling is against their religion and that they will go to hell. They may have even been told God wants the abuse to happen. Deep fundamental religious beliefs and abuse from within that religion are incredibly hard for a child to understand or process. This can lead to religious institutional grooming."

Via interviews in 2022, victims (who have requested to remain anonymous) have shared other reasons they did not tell:

They may feel ashamed or guilty and blame themselves.

They may perceive they will ruin the family or cause a divorce.

They may be involved in human trafficking and are unable to tell safe adults.

They may lack the ability to tell because they don't know anybody and don't trust anyone.

They fear that telling might make it worse.

They are terrified and paralyzed in fear.

They don't want anybody to know because they think it will reflect poorly on the family.

They are trying to protect siblings.

They did tell, but a primary caregiver or safe adult did not believe them, so they stopped telling.

They think that too many years have passed and it is too late to tell.

They have no safe adults.

We can all help prevent and protect children by teaching them about body-safety rules, consent, and prevention strategies. An educated and empowered child is a less attractive target to an abuser and is more likely to report a problem or incident. Parents, guardians, and other safe adults are essential parts of the prevention toolbox. One of your tools is knowing the signs.

Signs of Possible Sexual Abuse

Usually, there is no obvious sign that a child is being abused. In fact, in 95 percent of child sexual abuse cases, the child exhibits no physical signs (Adams et al., 2016). However, when there are physical signs, they may include redness, itching, rashes, swelling, bruising, or cuts in the genital area. The child may develop a urinary tract infection, abdominal pain, genital bleeding, yeast infections, or sexually transmitted diseases or begin bed-wetting. Sometimes, there may be rashes around the mouth or sores around the lips and inside the mouth. Because there are rarely any physical signs, we have to focus on the sometimes-subtle emotional signs and notice changes in behavior. For example, a child who is being abused may exhibit anxiety, depression, withdrawal, unexplained anger, mood swings, or sadness.

A child may engage in the use of sexual language that is not age-appropriate or in the child's everyday vocabulary. A child may begin engaging in new sexual behaviors. Sometimes, a child suddenly will begin avoiding a particular family member or friend's house. A child may begin avoiding an activity they once loved. They may engage in isolating behaviors such as spending a lot of time alone in the bedroom. Some children change their eating habits or friend groups. Some start dressing differently or causing trouble at school. Some engage in attention-seeking behavior.

In preschool and early childhood settings, this might present in different ways. For example, a child who is usually quiet and passive becomes suddenly aggressive and starts hitting and fighting with other children. A child may make frequent trips to the nurse or the bathroom. These are signs that can be missed but are worth noticing and paying attention to. Keep an eye out for these little changes, and connect with a child to provide support. Ask supportive, gentle questions as you try to figure out what is going on. Ask for help from your director or principal, and connect with the child's parents for assistance.

If you notice changes in a child's behavior or emotions, you can ask some simple questions such as the following:

- "I noticed that your stomach has been bothering you lately. Are you okay? Does it hurt anywhere else?"

- "I noticed that you don't want to go play at Tommy's house anymore. Is everything okay? What did you boys do at his house last week? Did anything fun happen? Did anybody get in trouble?"

- "Did anybody ask you to break a safety rule or keep a secret?"

Children don't usually come right out with a report if they have been sexually abused, especially if they are confused, embarrassed, or think they might get in trouble. You might hear some vague statements like, "I don't feel good," or "I have a terrible stomachache." And sometimes children keep this to themselves and say nothing. More often than not, there may be no signs at all.

How to Handle a Report without Freaking Out

When a child reports sexual abuse to you, I advise you to remain calm, but staying calm will not be your first reaction. It is almost impossible to be calm, especially if your own child comes to you and reports an incident of sexual abuse or inappropriate touch.

I remember picking my son up from the sleepover so many years ago. He came running out the door, jumped into my arms, and told me right away that he had had a red flag. The rage I felt inside, the blame I felt, the anger that bubbled up intensely inside my veins was almost impossible to handle. And I did not remain calm. I didn't know that I was supposed to be calm.

I did not expect this report at all. I thought that my children were safe and well supervised at my friend's house. We had been friends for so many years. How did I not sense that she would not supervise my children as closely as I did?

I was mad. I was angry. I was a mama bear.

I went inside and confronted the mother, the child, and the family about the accusations that my son had just shared outside our car. I was angry that this woman did not care for my son the way that I cared for him. I was angry that this woman did not let my child call me. I felt so guilty. I was angry with myself that I had let my child sleep at his friend's house, even though it was technically an emergency. This disclosure from my son triggered an intense emotional reaction and brought back every memory of my college sexual assaults and an incident from my childhood. I can't go back and fix my reaction, but I am sharing this with you because I hope you can stay calmer than I did.

You need to stay calm because, when a child discloses, it takes all of their strength and bravery. When they tell you, you must take a deep breath and listen carefully. Any type of anger or emotional outburst on your part will shut down the disclosure. If you get angry, start threatening to kill people, start yelling, or start saying you're going to call the police, your child will stop talking. Some children may even recant the story.

Your job is to listen and provide comfort. If your child or a student discloses any type of abuse to you, simply listen and thank them for telling. Reassure them that it is not their fault. "Thank you for telling me. I believe you. I will help you. It is not your fault." You can ask a few open-ended questions, such as "What happened then?" or say, "Tell me more." When the child is done sharing the story, thank them, tell them they're brave, tell them you love them, and then act responsibly and get the child to safety.

Responsible adults are required to report sexual abuse to the authorities, and if you're a teacher, you're a mandated reporter. You do not have to have proof. Make sure you know how to report sexual abuse if you are a disclosure recipient. Every school should have a sexual-abuse prevention policy and mission statement. The policy should include a procedure for teachers regarding what they should do if they receive a disclosure. When I received my first disclosure at kindergarten when I was a first-year teacher, I was unaware of any sexual-abuse prevention policy, but I used my common sense. I immediately called the school nurse and the principal.

Every school, whether it is a private school, home school, or public school, should have a system of reporting. Sexual-abuse prevention policies and procedures protect children. Whether you are a parent, guardian, or educator, take a minute to ask your school administrator for the policy. They should be able to provide a document that outlines the prevention policy and procedures in place that the school follows. If they do not have a policy, they need one. You can find a sample policy here: https://www.justicecenter.ny.gov/system/files/documents/2019/02/abusepreventionsamplepolicy.pdf

You can learn more about the requirements for mandated reporting and whom to contact in each state here: https://www.childwelfare.gov/topics/systemwide/laws-policies/statutes/manda/

After a child has disclosed abuse to you and you have made sure the child is safe, there are some things you can do to help the child.

- **Listen:** Some children will want to talk about their experience or red-flag scare.

- **Be present:** Make sure you are present and actively listening.

- **Be supportive:** Let the child know you are so proud of them for telling you.

- **Believe them:** Make sure the child knows you believe them and this was not their fault.

- **Journal:** Provide a journal for drawing and writing. Some children are not talkers. They may prefer writing and drawing out their emotions.

- **Walk and talk:** Get outside and move your bodies. Chat, talk, walk, and be available.

- **Seek therapy:** As a parent or guardian, find a great therapist who specializes in trauma work. Art, music, and play therapy are especially helpful.

- **Give time:** Spend extra time with them, and give extra love and support.

- **Communicate:** As a parent or guardian, try to let the child's teacher know what is going on so a backup layer of support and an extra set of eyes is available for the child.

- **Spend time with your pets:** As a parent or guardian, sometimes nothing feels better than a snuggle with the family pup or kitty or iguana or—you get the idea. A service dog really helped my son.

✗ ✗ ✗

As an aware and informed parent, guardian, caregiver, or educator, you can help prevent sexual abuse. We have the ability and duty to protect children from harm and ensure their safety. Protecting children involves more than just learning all of these facts and prevention strategies. It also means getting involved, speaking up, and engaging.

If a child does have an incident, they will know to tell you right away because they will know with 100 percent certainty that it is not their fault. You will be ready to help and support that child immediately. Our ability to teach, empower, and support children as they develop into young and thriving adults is critical. With this power comes a responsibility to educate, engage, and protect children not only with our words but also with our actions. As adults who love and protect children, our job is the most important job in the world.

Body Safety for Young Children: Empowering Caring Adults

Appendix: Resources

Alexandra Gucci Children's Foundation

https://www.alexandragucci.org/

Resources for families with a mission to free all children from sexual abuse

An Athlete's Silence

https://anathletessilence.com/

Helps organizations and individuals recognize the signs of grooming and sexual abuse and assists survivors of abuse

5 Waves

https://www.5waves.org

Information and support for those affected by sibling sexual abuse

Amazing Me

https://www.amazingme.com.au/

Australia-based organization offering resources on sexual health education for families and schools

American Society for the Positive Care of Children

https://americanspcc.org/sexual-child-abuse/

Resources and network for parents

Bark

https://www.bark.us/

Sells products for monitoring children's online activity

The Bayar Group

https://www.thebayargroup.com

Offers services, training, and consultation on creating safe spaces for children; helps organizations develop best practices to protect children

Bikers Against Child Abuse International

http://bacaworld.org/

Bikers and prevention advocates who lend support and work with local and state officials; B.A.C.A. raises funds to support the prevention of child abuse, and members speak out nationally and regionally against child abuse

The Body Boss Bootcamp

https://tough-topics-mom.mykajabi.com/body-boss-bootcamp

Kimberly King's child-friendly course on body safety

Body Safety Songs

https://www.youtube.com/@bodysafetysongs

Child-friendly songs about body safety

Buddy Speaks

https://buddyspeaks.org/

Organization provides preventative education and awareness to help end childhood sexual abuse

Cactus Foundation

https://cactusfoundation.org

India-based organization promoting healthy gender roles and combatting child sexual abuse

Childhelp

https://www.childhelp.org/contact/

"Childhelp exists to meet the physical, emotional, educational and spiritual needs of abused, neglected and at-risk children. We focus our efforts on advocacy, intervention, treatment, prevention, family resilience and community outreach."

Child Molestation Research and Prevention Institute

http://www.childmolestationprevention.org/

A national science-based nonprofit organization dedicated to preventing child sexual abuse through research, education, and family support

Child Rescue Coalition

https://childrescuecoalition.org/educations/avoid-these-predator-attracting-hashtags-to-keep-your-kids-safe-online/

List of predator-attracting hashtags to avoid

Child Welfare Information Gateway

https://www.childwelfare.gov

Offers a wide array of information on preventing child abuse and supporting families

Consent Parenting

https://www.consentparenting.com

Resources for parents on teaching children body safety, boundaries, and consent

C. Thomas Works

https://www.iamcthomas.net/

Offers workshops for educators on preventing, recognizing, and reacting responsibly to child sexual abuse; offers Writing to Wellness Workshops for survivors

CyberFareedah

https://www.cyberfareedah.com/

Teaches parents and caregivers how to keep children safer online

Darkness to Light

https://www.d2l.org/

An international sexual-abuse prevention and education organization with comprehensive research, educational programs, and resources for all adults who care for children

Defend Young Minds

https://www.defendyoungminds.com/

Dedicated to keeping children safe from the harms of pornography and online risks; provides families with books and other instructional resources

EducateEmpowerKids

https://educateempowerkids.org/

A collection of resources that empower young children, created by Jayneen Sanders; topics include body safety, self-esteem, and emotional wellness for children

Elizabeth Smart Foundation

https://www.elizabethsmartfoundation.org/

Works to educate to prevent sexual assault and to advocate for and bring healing to victims of sexual assault

Enough Abuse

https://enoughabuse.org/

"A citizen education and community mobilization initiative working to prevent child sexual abuse in our homes, schools, youth organizations and communities."

Gabb
https://gabb.com/
Sells products for monitoring children's online activity

Human Trafficking Hotline
https://humantraffickinghotline.org/en/report-trafficking
1-888-373-7888
Or text the National Human Trafficking Hotline at 233733

Joyful Heart Foundation
https://www.joyfulheartfoundation.org
Organization supporting abuse survivors and advocating for protection against violence and abuse

Kimberly King
https://www.kimberlykingbooks.com/best-books-for-kids
Recommended children's books on body safety
Resources for parents on tough topics, including sexual abuse, divorce, and self-esteem
Purchase books, online classes, and consultations

Lauren's Kids
https://laurenskids.org/
Resources for schools, families, and communities on preventing child sexual abuse and support for survivors

Monique Burr Foundation for Children
https://www.mbfpreventioneducation.org
Offers programs that help protect children from bullying, digital dangers, abuse, and exploitation

Mothers of Sexually Abused Children
https://www.mosac.net/
Resources and support for mothers whose children have experienced sexual abuse

National Center for Missing and Exploited Children
https://www.missingkids.org/education
Assistance, support, and education for victims, families, and community organizations

National Center on Safe Supportive Learning Environments

https://safesupportivelearning.ed.gov

Provides information for families and communities

National Center on Sexual Exploitation

https://endsexualexploitation.org

Offers information and resources

National Sexual Assault Telephone Hotline

https://www.rainn.org/about-national-sexual-assault-telephone-hotline

800.656.HOPE (4673)

Information and support from trained team members

National Sexual Violence Resource Center

https://www.nsvrc.org/

Information for survivors, family, friends, advocates, and educators

Parenting Safe Children

https://parentingsafechildren.com/

Sells workshops and resources to parents about body safety and prevention

Rape, Abuse, Incest National Network

www.rainn.org

Provides comprehensive resources, victim services, survivor stories, 24/7 hotline

Rescue America Human Trafficking Hotline

https://rescueamerica.ngo/

833-599-FREE

Works to rescue and empower the sexually exploited

The Rowan Center

https://www.therowancenter.org

Offers resources to people in Connecticut who experience sexual assault

Safe from Online Sex Abuse

https://sosatogether.org/

Raises awareness and combats online child sex abuse and exploitation

Safely Ever After

https://safelyeverafter.com/

Up-to-date information and prevention education programs to help empower families against child predators

Sex Ed Rescue

https://sexedrescue.com

Advice and training for parents and guardians on teaching children about sexual development

Stop It Now!

https://www.stopitnow.org

1.888.PREVENT

Services, education, and support in stopping child sexual abuse

Stop the Demand Project

https://www.stopthedemandproject.com/

Combats human-rights abuses through technology

Survivors Network of Those Abused by Priests

https://www.snapnetwork.org

Support for survivors of abuse by ministers, priests, nuns, or rabbis; protecting children and the vulnerable; educating the public

Tell Somebody

https://tellsomebodytoday.com/index.html

Works to prevent child abuse through awareness and workshops

Tim Tebow Foundation

https://www.timtebowfoundation.org/

Fights against human trafficking and child exploitation

U.S. Center for Safesport

https://uscenterforsafesport.org/

Dedicated to ending sexual, physical, and emotional abuse of athletes

References and Recommended Reading

Adams, Joyce A., et al. 2016. "Updated Guidelines for the Medical Assessment and Care of Children Who May Have Been Sexually Abused." *Journal of Pediatric and Adolescent Gynecology* 29(2): 81–87.

Alyse, Shari. 2019. *Love Yourself Happy: A Journey Back to You.* Wellness Ink Publishing.

American Academy of Pediatrics. 2019. "Sexual Behaviors in Young Children: What's Normal, What's Not?" HealthyChildren.org. https://www.healthychildren.org/English/ages-stages/preschool/Pages/Sexual-Behaviors-Young-Children.aspx

Ardiel, Evan, and Catharine Rankin. 2010. "The Importance of Touch in Development." *Paediatric Child Health* 15(3): 153–156.

Assink, Mark, et al. 2019. "Risk Factors for Child Sexual Abuse Victimization: A Meta-Analytic Review." *Psychological Bulletin* 145(5): 459–489.

Auxier, Brooke, Monica Anderson, Andrew Perrin, and Erica Turner. 2020. "Parenting Children in the Age of Screens." Pew Research Center. https://www.pewresearch.org/internet/2020/07/28/parenting-children-in-the-age-of-screens/

Bark. 2021. "What Is Discord and Is It Safe? A Discord App Review for Parents." Bark. https://www.bark.us/app-reviews/apps/discord/#:~:text=to%20be%20kids.-,Positive%20Value%20%F0%9F%92%99,while%20playing%20video%20games%20together

Beer, Sophie. 2018. *Love Makes a Family.* New York: Dial Books for Young Readers.

Bethell, Christina, et al. 2019. "Positive Childhood Experiences and Adult Mental and Relational Health in a Statewide Sample: Associations Across Adverse Childhood Experiences Levels." *JAMA Pediatrics* 173(11): e193007. https://doi.org/10.1001/jamapediatrics.2019.3007

Bernstein, Gabrielle. 2022. *Happy Days: The Guided Path from Trauma to Profound Freedom and Inner Peace*. Carlsbad, CA: Hay House.

Bottoms, Bette, Aaron Rudnick, and Michelle Epstein. 2007. "A Retrospective Study of Factors Affecting the Disclosure of Childhood Sexual Abuse and Physical Abuse." In *Child Sexual Abuse: Disclosure, Delay, and Denial*. New York: Routledge.

Block, Stephanie D., and Linda M. Williams. 2019. *Prosecution of Child Sexual Abuse: A Partnership to Improve Outcomes*. National Criminal Justice Reference Service, Office of Justice Programs. https://www.ojp.gov/pdffiles1/nij/grants/252768.pdf

Bourke, Ashling, et al. 2014. "Female Perpetrators of Child Sexual Abuse: Characteristics of the Offender and Victim." *Psychology, Crime, and Law* 20(8). https://doi.org/10.1080/1068316X.2013.860456

Bowlby John. 1982. *Attachment*. Vol 1. of Attachment and Loss. 2nd edition. New York: Basic Books.

Brewster, Thomas. 2022. "Scammers Are Extorting Parents with Their Dead Children's Nude Images, FBI Says." November 10. *Forbes*. https://www.forbes.com/sites/thomasbrewster/2022/11/10/scammers-are-extorting-parents-with-their-dead-childrens-nude-images-fbi-says/?sh=4433c043efb1

Broman-Fulks, Joshua J., et al. 2007. "Sexual Assault Disclosure in Relation to Adolescent Mental Health: Results from the National Survey of Adolescents." *Journal of Clinical Child and Adolescent Psychology* 36(2): 260–266.

Bruner, Hannah. 2021. *What Makes a Family?* Colorado: Hannah Bruner.

Canter, Lee. 2009. *Assertive Discipline: Positive Behavior Management for Today's Classroom*. 4th edition. Bloomington, IN: Solution Tree Press.

Child Rescue Coalition. 2023. "Avoid These Predator-Attracting Hashtags." Child Rescue Coalition. https://childrescuecoalition.org/educations/avoid-these-predator-attracting-hashtags-to-keep-your-kids-safe-online/

Conte, Jon R., Steven Wolf, and Tim Smith. 1989. "What Sexual Offenders Tell Us About Prevention Strategies." *Child Abuse and Neglect* 13(2): 293–301.

Coyne, Sarah, Adam Rogers, Jane Shawcroft, and Jeffrey Hurst. 2021. "Dressing up with Disney and Make-Believe with Marvel: The Impact of Gendered Costumes on Gender Typing, Prosocial Behavior, and Perseverance during Early Childhood." *Sex Roles* 85(5–6): 301–312.

Craig, Eleanor. 2022. "Teaching Safeguarding through Books: A Content Analysis of Child Sexual Abuse Prevention Books." *Journal of Child Sexual Abuse* 31(3): 257–275.

Cunningham, Patricia M. 2016. *Phonics They Use: Words for Reading and Writing*. 7th edition. Hoboken, NJ: Pearson.

Darkness to Light. 2023. "Identifying Child Sexual Abuse." Darkness to Light. https://www.d2l.org/get-help/identifying-abuse/

Day, Andrew, Katie Thurlow, and Jessica Woolliscroft. 2003. "Working with Childhood Sexual Abuse: A Survey of Mental Health Professionals." *Child Abuse and Neglect* 27(2): 191–198.

Doak-Gebauer, Charlene E. 2019. *The Internet: Are Children in Charge? Theory of Digital Supervision*. Victoria, BC: Tellwell Talent.

Dube, Shanta R., et al. 2005. "Long-Term Consequences of Childhood Sexual Abuse by Gender of the Victim." *American Journal of Preventive Medicine* 28(5): 430–437.

Elliott, Michele, Kevin Browne, and Jennifer Kilcoyne. 1995. "Child Sexual Abuse Prevention: What Offenders Tell Us." *Child Abuse and Neglect* 19(5): 579–594.

Federal Bureau of Investigation. n.d. "How We Can Help You." https://www.fbi.gov/how-we-can-help-you/safety-resources/scams-and-safety/common-scams-and-crimes/sextortion

Fererro, Jenny, and Rebecca Bishop. 2022. *Guidance for Supporting Gender Diversity in Early Childhood Education*. Lewisville, NC: Gryphon House.

Finkelhor, David. 1994. "Current Information on the Scope and Nature of Child Sexual Abuse." *The Future of Children* 4(2): 31–53.

Finkelhor, David, and Anne Shattuck. 2012. *Characteristics of Crimes against Juveniles*. Durham, NH: Crimes against Children Research Center, University of New Hampshire. https://www.unh.edu/ccrc/sites/default/files/media/2022-03/characteristics-of-crimes-against-juveniles_0.pdf

Gewirtz-Meydan, Ateret, and David Finkelhor. 2020. "Sexual Abuse and Assault in a Large National Sample of Children and Adolescents." *Child Maltreatment* 25(2): 203–214. https://doi.org/10.1177/1077559519873975

Greene-Colozzi, Emily A., Georgia M. Winters, Brandy Blasko, and Elizabeth L. Jeglic. 2020. "Experiences and Perceptions of Online Sexual Solicitation and Grooming of Minors: A Retrospective Report." *Journal of Child Sexual Abuse* 29(7): 836–854.

Hancox, Robert J., Barry J. Milne, and Richie Poulton. 2004. "Association between Child and Adolescent Television Viewing and Adult Health: A Longitudinal Birth Cohort Study." *Lancet* 364(9430): 257–262.

Harris, Robie H. 2012. *Who's in My Family? All about Our Families.* Somerville, MA: Candlewick Press.

Internet Watch Foundation. 2020. "The Dark Side of the Selfie: IWF Partners with the Marie Collins Foundation in New Campaign to Call on Young Men to Report Self-Generated Sexual Images of Under 18s." Internet Watch Foundation. https://www.iwf.org.uk/news-media/news/the-dark-side-of-the-selfie-iwf-partners-with-the-marie-collins-foundation-in-new-campaign-to-call-on-young-men-to-report-self-generated-sexual-images-of-under-18s/

Jenson, Kristen A. 2017. *Good Pictures, Bad Pictures Jr.: A Simple Plan to Protect Young Minds.* Richland, WA: Glen Cove Press.

Jenson, Kristen A. 2018. *Good Pictures, Bad Pictures: Porn-Proofing Today's Young Kids.* 2nd edition. Richland, WA: Glen Cove Press.

Jones, Lisa, et al. 2012. "Prevalence and Risk of Violence against Children with Disabilities: A Systematic Review and Meta-Analysis of Observational Studies." *Lancet* 380(9845): 899–907.

Kendler, Kenneth, et al. 2000. "Childhood Sexual Abuse and Adult Psychiatric and Substance Use Disorders in Women: An Epidemiological and Cotwin Control Analysis." *Archives of General Psychiatry* 57(10): 953–959.

King, Kimberly. 2016. "The 3 Big Red Flags of Sexual Abuse." Defend Young Minds. https://www.defendyoungminds.com/post/3-big-red-flags-sexual-abuse

King, Zack, and Kimberly King. 2020. *I Said NO! A Kid-to-Kid Guide to Keeping Private Parts Private*. Weaverville, CA: Boulden Publishing.

Klapper, Rebecca A. 2021. "High School Football Team Accused of Sexual Assault on 2 Freshmen in Locker Room." August 23. *Newsweek*. https://www.newsweek.com/ high-school-football-team-accused-sexual-assault-2-freshmen-locker-room-1622247?amp=1

Krienert, Jessie, and Jeffrey Walsh. 2011. "Sibling Sexual Abuse: An Empirical Analysis of Offender, Victim, and Event Characteristics in National Incident-Based Reporting System (NIBRS) Data, 2000–2007." *Journal of Child Sexual Abuse* 20(4): 353–372.

Lahtinen, Hanna-Mari, Aarno Laitila, Julia Korkman, and Noora Ellonen. 2018. "Children's Disclosures of Sexual Abuse in a Population-Based Sample. *Child Abuse and Neglect* 76(1): 84–94. https://doi.org/10.1016/j.chiabu.2017.10.011

Lemaigre, Charlotte, Emily Taylor, and Claire Gittoes. 2017. "Barriers and Facilitators to Disclosing Sexual Abuse in Childhood and Adolescence: A Systematic Review." *Child Abuse and Neglect*, 70: 39–52. https://doi.org/10.1016/j.chiabu.2017.05.009

Lester, Stuart, and Wendy Russell. 2010. *Children's Right to Play: An Examination of the Importance of Play in the Lives of Children Worldwide*. The Hague, Netherlands: Bernard van Leer Foundation. https://files.eric.ed.gov/fulltext/ED522537.pdf

Leung, Alexander K. C., and William Lane M. Robson. 1993. "Childhood Masturbation." *Clinical Pediatrics* 32(4): 238–241.

London, Kamala, Maggie Bruck, Stephen Ceci, and Daniel Shuman. 2005. "Disclosure of Child Sexual Abuse: What Does the Research Tell Us about the Ways That Children Tell?" *Psychology, Public Policy, and Law* 11(1): 194–226.

Madigan, Sheri, et al. 2019. "Association between Screen Time and Children's Performance on a Developmental Screening Test." *JAMA Pediatrics* 173(3): 244–250.

Mannello, Marianne, Theresa Casey, and Cathy Atkinson. 2020. "Article 31: Play, Leisure and Recreation." In *The International Handbook on Child Rights and School Psychology*. New York: Springer Science and Business Media.

Meta. 2023. "Help Center: Parental Supervision." Instagram. https://help.instagram.com/ 309877544512275

Michaelis, Richard, and Gerhard Niemann. 2004. *Entwicklungsneurologie und Neuropädiatrie [Developmental Neurology and Neuropediatrics]*. Leipzig, Germany: Georg Thieme Verlag.

Mooney, Carol Garhart. 2010. *Theories of Attachment: An Introduction to Bowlby, Ainsworth, Gerber, Brazelton, Kennell, and Klaus*. St. Paul, MN: Redleaf.

Morse, Dan, and Donna St. George. 2019. "A Football Locker Room, a Broomstick, and A Sex Assault Case Roil a School." March 29. *The Washington Post*. https://www.washingtonpost.com/local/crime/a-football-locker-room-a-broomstick-and-a-sex-assault-case-roil-a-school/2019/03/29/01500f30-2fc8-11e9-8ad3-9a5b113ecd3c_story.html

Mutavi, Teresia, et al. 2018. "Incidence of Self-Esteem among Children Exposed to Sexual Abuse in Kenya." *Global Social Welfare: Research, Policy and Practice* 5(1): 39–47. https://doi.org/10.1007/s40609-017-0107-3

National Center for Missing and Exploited Children. 2022. CyberTipline 2021 Report. https://www.missingkids.org/gethelpnow/cybertipline/cybertiplinedata

Newman, Leslea. 2016. *Heather Has Two Mommies*. Somerville, MA: Candlewick Press.

Poulain, Tanja, et al. 2018. "Reciprocal Associations between Electronic Media Use and Behavioral Difficulties in Preschoolers." *International Journal of Environmental Research and Public Health* 15(4): 814.

RAINN. 2023. "Child Sexual Abuse." RAINN. https://www.rainn.org/articles/child-sexual-abuse#:~:text=What%20is%20child%20sexual%20abuse,on%20the%20victim%20for%20years

Richardson, Justin, and Peter Parnell. 2015. *And Tango Makes Three*. New York: Little Simon Books.

Rideout, Vicky. 2016. "Measuring Time Spent with Media: The Common Sense Census of Media Use by US 8- To 18-Year-Olds." *Journal of Children and Media* 10(1): 138–144.

Rideout, Vicky, Alanna Peebles, Supreet Mann, and Michael B. Robb. 2021. *Common Sense Census: Media Use by Teens and Tweens*. San Francisco, CA: Common Sense. https://www.commonsensemedia.org/sites/default/files/research/report/8-18-census-integrated-report-final-web_0.pdf

Rohde, Paul, et al. 2008. "Associations of Child Sexual and Physical Abuse with Obesity and Depression in Middle-Aged Women." *Child Abuse and Neglect* 32(9): 878– 887.

Rotner, Shelley, and Sheila Kelly. 2015. *Families*. New York: Holiday House.

Russell, Helen. 2021. "Lego to Remove Gender Bias from Its Toys after Findings of Child Survey." *The Guardian*, October 10. https://www.theguardian.com/lifeandstyle/2021/oct/11/lego-to-remove-gender-bias-after-survey-shows-impact-on-children-stereotypes

Sedlak, Andrea J., et al. 2010. *Fourth National Incidence Study of Child Abuse and Neglect (NIS–4): Report to Congress, Executive Summary*. Washington, DC: U.S. Department of Health and Human Services, Administration for Children and Families. https://www.acf.hhs.gov/sites/default/files/documents/opre/nis4_report_exec_summ_pdf_jan2010.pdf

Shaheed, Fareedah. 2022. Kids Safe Movement. CyberFareedah.com. https://www.cyberfareedah.com/

Studer, Cathy. 2019. *Broken to Beautifully Whole: A Compelling Crusade to Break the Silence, Move through the Trauma, and Heal the Pain*. Columbus, OH: Author Academy Elite.

Townsend, Catherine. 2013. *Prevalence and Consequences of Child Sexual Abuse Compared with Other Childhood Experiences*. Charleston, SC: Darkness to Light. https://www.d2l.org/wp-content/uploads/2016/10/most-significant-severe-longterm-paper-D2L.pdf

Townsend, Catherine, Alyssa Rheingold, and M. Lyndon Haviland. 2016. *Estimating a Child Sexual Abuse Prevalence Rate for Practitioners: An Updated Review of Child Sexual Abuse Prevalence Studies*. Charleston, SC: Darkness to Light. https://www.d2l.org/wp-content/uploads/2020/01/Updated-Prevalence-White-Paper-1-25-2016_2020.pdf

Twenge, Jean M., and W. Keith Campbell. 2018. "Associations between Screen Time and Lower Psychological Well-Being among Children and Adolescents: Evidence from a Population-Based Study." *Preventative Medicine Reports* 12: 271–283.

Ullman, Sarah E. 2007. "Relationship to Perpetrator, Disclosure, Social Reactions, and PTSD Symptoms in Child Sexual Abuse Survivors." *Journal of Child Sexual Abuse* 16(1): 19–36.

US Center for SafeSport. 2022. "2020 Athlete Culture and Climate Survey." US Center for SafeSport. https://uscenterforsafesport.org/survey-results/

Waters, Everett, and E. Mark Cummings. 2000. "A Secure Base from Which to Explore Close Relationships." *Child Development* 71(1): 164–172.

Index

Fear, 115, 164, 171

Feelings, 115–121

Female predators, 35

G

Gender, 35, 55–58, 105

Gift giving, 23, 149

Grooming, 18–29, 49–50, 88, 166–169

Guilt, 115, 164, 171

H

Handling a report of sexual abuse,
    173–175

Hands in the pants, 59–61

Healthy sexual-abuse prevention climate,
    82–83

Healthy touch, 52–55

Human trafficking, 171, 180

I

"I" statements, 43–44

If/then statements, 150

Imitating adult sexual acts, 67

J

Journals, 33–34, 116–117, 175

L

Labeling, 56–57

Line of sight, 69–70

Listening, 34, 130–131, 174–175

Low self-esteem, 115

M

Making an emergency exit, 160–163

Mandatory reporting, 39, 108, 174

Masturbation, 59–61, 66

Memory suppression, 170

Misconceptions, 11, 13–16, 35

Modesty, 65

N

"No secrets" rule, 47–48

Nonbinary children, 55–56, 83

O

Obscene language, 67

Online grooming, 23–25, 88

Online safety, 86–103, 147–148

Open-door policy, 83

Open-ended questions, 116–117

P

Parents/guardians. *See also* Families
  communication with teachers, 54
  family online safety contract, 92
  frequently asked questions from, 55–59
  live-in partners, 25
  online safety tips, 88–100
  single mothers, 28–29
  talking with children about technology, 89–93

Playdates, 15, 42–47, 77–78, 159

Playing doctor, 59, 159

Playing dress-up, 55–56

Pornography, 87–88, 101, 159

Posting pictures of children, 14–15, 93–95

Potty emergencies, 71–76, 136

Potty training, 61, 65, 125–128, 136, 141–142, 144–145

Praise, 24, 150

Protective factors, 45–46

Q

Questions
  about child behavior, 52–69
  asking children, 32
  children ask about sex, 105–106
  from children, 64–65

  from parents, 55–59
  from teachers, 59–64
  open-ended, 116–117
  to ask children after a playdate, 44–45
  to ask if you see signs of sexual abuse, 172–173
  to ask schools and organizations, 19–20
  to ask yourself about playdates, 43

R

Reasons children don't tell, 170–171

Red flag behaviors, 7, 18–29, 49–50, 143–148

Red-flag mailboxes, 70

Rule of three, 22

Rule of two, 71–74, 136

S

Safe adults, 30–31

Safer sports and activities, 81–85

Safety chats, 32

Safety circles, 30–40

Security cameras, 38

Sensitivity to cultural or personal beliefs, 44, 145–147

Sex education, 15–16

Sextortion, 95

Sexual predators, 2, 13, 16–17, 35, 115